An Honest Preface
and Other Essays

Books by Walter Prescott Webb

The Great Plains

The Texas Rangers

Divided We Stand

The Great Frontier

More Water for Texas

An Honest Preface and Other Essays

An Honest Preface
and Other Essays

by Walter Prescott Webb

with an appreciative introduction

by Joe B. Frantz

BOSTON

HOUGHTON MIFFLIN COMPANY

THE RIVERSIDE PRESS CAMBRIDGE

1 9 5 9

First printing

Acknowledgments

T HE TRADITIONAL ARTICLES from the traditional historical journals will not be found in the pages ahead, for the man who wrote the pieces is not a traditional historian. What follows is intended more as a representative sampling of the shorter works of Walter Prescott Webb than as an attempt to be inclusive or especially significant. Many of Webb's more important articles have appeared later in modified form as chapters in his books; such articles have not been included.

Since Webb is a haphazard records keeper where his own career is concerned, I have had to lean heavily on others in collecting the information and even the articles which follow. In the pursuit I have incurred debts of varying degree to Mr. John Haller, Mr. Joe Small, Mr. Charles E. Green, Judge James P. Hart, Mr. J. Frank Dobie, and Mr. Robert Pool, all of Austin; to President Logan Wilson, Vice-President Harry H. Ransom, Dean J. Alton Burdine, Mr. Roy Bedichek, Professor Archibald R. Lewis of the Department of History, Mr. Frank Wardlaw of the University of Texas Press, Dr. Llerena Friend of the

Eugene C. Barker Texas History Center — all of the University of Texas; to Mr. Dorman H. Winfrey, Archivist of the Texas State Library; to Miss Helaine Nickum of Waco; to Dr. E. C. Barksdale of Arlington State College; to Mr. George Fuermann of the Houston *Post*; to Dr. Rupert N. Richardson of Hardin-Simmons University; to Mr. Fred Gipson of Mason, Texas; to Professor William Ransom Hogan of Tulane University; to Mr. Joe Wiley of Dallas; and to Dr. W. Eugene Hollon of the University of Oklahoma. Much of the material concerning Webb's relationship with the Texas State Historical Association came from an M.A. thesis by Mr. Tom Bowman Brewer, "A History of the Department of History of the University of Texas, 1883-1951," written in 1956. The Graduate Research Institute of the University of Texas, presided over by Dean W. Gordon Whaley, assisted me mightily. Particularly I want to thank Miss Colleen T. Kain and my wife Helen for services that ranged from proofreading and typing to rearranging their hours to fit my often disordered schedule.

JOE B. FRANTZ

Contents

An Appreciative Introduction

by Joe B. Frantz

Walter Prescott Webb: "He'll Do to Ride the River With"

H E WAS sixteen years old, and he hated farming. He liked to read, but in West Texas at the turn of the century there was very little to read. What there was he had read over and over.

Walter Prescott Webb's father was a Stephens County teacher and farmer. Even today, the mere announcement that a man is a Stephens County farmer paints pictures, not altogether pleasant, in the minds of Texans who know that country between Fort Worth and Abilene. Despite Cadillacs and air-conditioned ranch houses and electric pumps and drilling rigs, Stephens County remains harsh and raw and spacious. Its trees are mesquites and post oak — their very pretension to being trees would strike a New Englander as ludicrous. The sun beats in the summer; the wind sweeps in the winter. It never rains; or if it does, it floods. To put the best face on it, Stephens County has amplitude. And to be honest, it was not a merry place to farm in 1900 — or in 1958.

Casner P. Webb, however, was a farmer with a difference. He read books. He also questioned orthodox beliefs and liked to be something of an icon-smasher. In odd moments he was a schoolteacher. He definitely sympathized with a craving for learning. But he had a family of five to feed, and Walter was the only boy, and farming in Stephens County was their way of life.

When Casner Webb wasn't admonishing Walter to do a better job behind his Georgia stock, he was telling him that there was a better life than theirs. The best life, the elder often said, belonged to the professional man. A bit contentious himself, he especially admired lawyers and hoped the boy would seek a legal career someday. The boy himself rather liked the idea of being a doctor. Actually, anything would be better than farming.

Every now and then his father would vary talk of Walter's future by telling him how great it would be to become an editor. Since the boy wasn't sure what an editor was, the idea intrigued him.

In the little outpost town of Ranger, Texas — so called because it was once a headquarters of the Texas Rangers — there worked an editor of a weekly newspaper. One day the boy rode into the Ranger *Record* office to see his ideal in the flesh and in action.

As shy then as he is now, he forced himself to enter the country newspaper office, where he stood awkwardly, looking at the man who was what he hoped to be. The editor, probably in a green eye shade, was pecking out a letter on an old Oliver, the first typewriter the boy had ever seen. Walter Webb shifted his weight and stared over the man's shoulder. Presently the editor felt that discomfort which comes when a stranger continues to peer silently and intently.

"What do you want, boy?" the great man asked.

"I wanted to see an editor," Walter Webb said.

"You've seen one," the editor retorted, and then turned

back to his Oliver. Walter Webb continued to stare. Meanwhile, out of the corner of his eye, he had spotted a sprawling pile of exchanges. But he kept his eyes riveted on the editor at work.

Irritated, the editor said, "You can go!" Young Webb, pointing to the exchanges, asked, "Can I have some of those?"

"Take all you want — the whole pile, but go!"

It was a windfall, the dream of a print-starved child's lifetime. It had begun to rain, but Walter Webb climbed aboard his horse and set out along the 9-mile trail to the farm, protecting his new riches as zealously as he could, except for the one paper he was reading as he rode. Despite the cold rain beating against his face, despite the inescapable farm at the end of the ride, despite a home short on material comforts, he would probably never approach closer to pure ecstasy in the more than half century that lay ahead. He had in his possession all the wealth in the world that evening — more reading than he could finish in the stolen moments of several days. And then he could start all over again.

One of the papers he read that night was the *Sunny South*, published in Atlanta and featuring, naturally enough, Joel Chandler Harris, as well as less local writers of equivalent caliber. The *Sunny South* was running a circulation promotion whereby for ten cents you could obtain a three-month subscription.

The family went to bed. All except Walter and his mother. In many ways Mary Kyle Webb was the traditional frontier wife and mother — faithful to her church, uncomplaining of her lot, gentle to her family, and forever at work. Tonight she was as busy as usual, so at first she did not notice that her son had failed to go to bed with the others.

"Hadn't you better go to bed, Walter?" she said a little later.

"Yes'm," he said. And continued to hang around, half embarrassed and all-determined, just as in the newspaper office earlier that day.

After a while, Mrs. Webb said, "What is it you want, Walter?"

He told her of the subscription offer, and for the second time that day a scene was etched that would never leave his memory. In the Webb family in Stephens County in those days, ten cents was hard to come by. Without a word his mother put down her work, walked over to a corner where she kept a sock, took out ten cents she had saved from somewhere, and handed it to her son.

The *Sunny South* had an active letters-to-the-editor column. One day Webb wrote the *Sunny South*, saying that he was a Texas farm boy who wanted to be a writer, but that he had only a meager education and no money. On one occasion he had gone three years without being able to attend school. For some reason, probably because it was so recognizably a youth's clumsily honest appeal for advice, the editor of the *Sunny South* printed the letter.

The boy signed the letter "Prescott" because he had noticed that some of the *Sunny South* correspondents used high-sounding literary pseudonyms. "Prescott" was about as high-sounding as he thought a Stephens County boy ought to get, but something with more tone than Walter Webb was definitely necessary, he figured.

"It was in the spring," Webb recalls, "and we were plowing corn in the new-cleared ground. The corn was about ten or twelve inches tall. We had come to the long hours of the late afternoon and had stopped to rest on the beams of the plows when my sister returned from the mailbox of the new rural route. She handed me a letter, the most marvelous I had ever seen. The envelope was of the finest paper, the handwriting bold and black on the glossy surface. It was sealed with red wax, stamped with the letter *H*. The only address was 'Prescott, Care Teacher, Ranger, Texas.' It reached me only because the postmaster, a Confederate veteran, read my *Sunny South* before I got it and was the only person aside from the postman who knew my middle name.

"The writer said he had seen my letter, that I should keep my mind fixed on an education. 'Remember,' he quoted, 'in the bright lexicon of youth there is no such word as fail.' He would like to send me something to read — if I would permit. Then he added that, on second thought, he was sending it anyway. The signature was 'William E. Hinds, 489 Classon Avenue, Brooklyn, New York.'

"Then came books on writing, and magazines, the best in the land: *The American Boy*, Joe Mitchell Chappell's *National*, devoted to Washington affairs, Lyman Abbott's *The Outlook*, Orson Swett Marden's *Success*, and others. He encouraged me to write letters of description and narration, and each Christmas came a letter and a tie that was in a class by itself in Stephens County.

"This relationship was unchanged for several years, until 1909 when I was teaching at the famous Merriman school with millions of dollars of oil hidden under the Baptist churchyard nearby. One bleak day in late January came a long letter asking many questions: Had I thought of going to college? Where? How much money had I saved? How much would be required at the college of my choice? And so on. I need not answer all the questions, but if I wanted to go to college, he would like to advance the funds needed after mine gave out. It might be, he explained, that in the future he would be proud to remember that he had had the privilege of helping, and I quote, Walter Prescott Webb.

"His letter resolved all indecision, and that fall I entered the University. At the end of two years I owed him about $500, and we decided that I should not go deeper in debt. I alternated between teaching and college and he always made it possible for me to finish any year I had started. One summer I made enough money to go to New York to see him, but he advised me not to spend it that way. I never saw him for he died in 1916 after I had graduated but before the debt was all paid. His sister spent the next winter with us in San Antonio, and from her I learned all I have ever known of this man."

Although Webb never met him, he felt a moral commitment to Hinds — in fact he still feels it. Hinds never knew of the return on his investment, but Webb, whose religion is deeply personal and not of the orthodox, churchgoing variety, hopes that somehow his benefactor knows that the investment has paid off.

Shortly after Hinds' death, his sister wrote Webb that her brother's estate had been settled and that among his papers were a number of notes from Walter Prescott Webb, each marked, "Paid in full." Actually by that time, Webb had paid off all but seventy-five dollars.

The team of Webb and Hinds somehow made it through college. Meanwhile Webb was progressing in teaching assignments, moving beyond the catch-as-catch-can one-room country schools in which he was janitor, teacher, and salary collector. He taught in accredited schools now, schools with nine-month terms. He was a principal at Cuero.

At Beeville, down in the huisache country of South Texas, he had been given the added assignment of tennis coach. No athlete himself, he had the good sense to stay out of the way of two talented performers who tried out for the squad. As both of them were left-handed, their opposition could seldom adjust its training in time to figure out where the ball was coming from. The result was that Webb's Beeville boys won the state doubles championship, and Webb was considered quite a coach by everyone except Walter Webb. Or as Webb put it, "Opportunities for left-handed tennis coaches were limited, so I didn't do any more coaching." One of the boys was Curtis Walker, who later enjoyed a long major league baseball career.

In a way these Beeville years were the happiest of his public-school teaching career. He liked the school and he liked the town. Back in Stephens County he had always been so busy counting the noses of his charges to see whether enough were still coming to keep the school — and himself — alive that he could never quite feel easy in his job.

By the time he had finished college, Webb had worked his way into a teaching job at Main High School in San Antonio.

In 1914 the United States underwent an economic recession that was eventually reversed by the outbreak of war in Europe. Walter Webb, never economically flush, was preparing to start his senior year at the University of Texas with exactly three silver dollars in his pocket. The head of the University's extension division got in touch with him, told him that the state normal school in San Marcos needed a man immediately and that Webb could probably have the job. Since his three dollars weren't enough for the round trip to San Marcos plus food and lodging, Webb borrowed $15 from a younger faculty friend. His clothes were on the run-down side, but it was too late to do anything about that, which must have hurt a man with Webb's sartorial pride.

He took the train to San Marcos, arriving at suppertime. Webb never cares for people who supplicate, and would never approach a prospective employer himself on a basis of need.

Accordingly, he took a room at the hotel, ate a leisurely dinner, called a two-horse carriage, and rode in style to the home of the college president. He had the carriage wait.

Fifteen minutes later he was outside, floating. He had a college job, at $150 a month! To a man who was now down past his last $3, and who had never made more than $100 a month previously, this was great expectations beyond anything dreamed by Dickens. He checked out of the hotel, caught an eleven o'clock train back to Austin, and drank coffee throughout the night.

"No other job and no other money ever thrilled me like that," Webb recalls.

It was quite a job. He taught two subjects — education and mathematics. About all he could do was hold on and try to stay a problem ahead of his students. He was a sort of assistant to the president, C. E. Evans, a sterling character but one of those bosses who never realize that their subordinates have a private life. Webb was acting registrar. He was also college bookkeeper.

"I didn't know a debit from a credit when I took the job," he confesses.

Fifteen, sixteen hours a day he put in, including Sundays. He felt that this was opportunity and he was prepared to work to make the most of it. At the end of the quarter the man he was replacing returned; and Webb trudged back for his senior year, but with the comforting feel of a bank account. He took the heaviest load of his undergraduate career and did his best work, and finished.

Before he had left San Marcos Webb had tried to balance the school's books. He was $3600 out of balance. For three days and nights he searched, despair deepening all the time. Then by chance he learned that President Evans had cashed a counter check for $3600 to pay some running expenses and

had forgotten to notify the college office. Webb left San
Marcos even.

"That was the last time I remember worrying," Webb
says. "Since then I have believed that things could be worked
out.

"Some people express a desire to relive their days when they
were young. I never wanted to go back, for the problems of
childhood can seem insoluble. You live so much more in-
tensely. I like the assurance of maturity."

And so Webb plodded slowly toward his goal. When he
finally attained his bachelor's degree, he was twenty-seven
years of age. The University of Texas had found him an indifferent student, for despite his ambition he refused to be
harnessed to the discipline of the classroom. It wasn't that he
rebelled openly — it was merely that however much he intended to carry out assignments, some book or magazine invariably appeared to throw his intentions off stride. The
course might be Shakespeare, and Webb might love Shakespeare, but not when it was assigned. *Hamlet* assigned would
never stand a chance against an unassigned latest volume of
O. Henry. The results were mediocre grades and a vast smat-
tering of information.

Actually, the student Webb's working habits were no different from the historian Webb's. He is in his seventies now,
and he can pound a typewriter with all the enthusiasm of a
sophomore out to save the world — and with considerable
more economy of effort. By nine o'clock in the morning the
rapid two-fingered clack of his typewriter comes floating out of
Garrison Hall 102, to be halted only by someone with a problem or an invitation to coffee. At eleven o'clock that night the
typewriter will be going as strong as ever in a now-still Garrison Hall. His pace is steady, never hurried, never impatient.

His application is the marvel of his younger colleagues, who yield to a weariness that he never seems to feel.

And yet if in a moment of weakness he accepts a commission for an article, he will circle it as warily as a dog investigating a porcupine, make a few trial runs, and delay actual involvement as long as possible. It never fails to startle his more traditional colleagues who are aware that Webb is fighting a deadline to find him at the beginning of the day with a new J. P. Marquand novel, and to find him the next night still reading the same novel, hardly having put it down for more than meals and sleep. He practically loses a half-day each week to the *Saturday Evening Post,* and another half day to *U. S. News & World Report,* which he dislikes editorially but reads consistently "because it tells you something."

But just as the student Webb could not be bound by assignments and could always be distracted by a book or magazine, so it is with the historian. He meets his deadlines — usually; but he is no tightly disciplined, single-minded, one-man historical factory. He works by spurts, and a spurt might last from one long day to a year or more. On the other hand, his interruptions might last just as long. He once went thirteen years between books, but in the meanwhile the novels he read, the thinking he did, the real estate he traded, and the Santa Gertrudis cattle he experimented with more than compensated — in his eyes — for the time lost. Certainly he will never be held up to the beginning student as an orderly working ideal.

At Main High School in San Antonio — Old Main, as it is invariably called today — where Webb continued to teach after his graduation, he was unhappy. He liked San Antonio, he had taken a wife, Jane Oliphant of Austin, and shortly he would have a daughter, to be named Mildred, on the way.

However, he and his superintendent were having a running disagreement, the reason for which has faded. As Webb wryly says, "One of us had to go, and he was the superintendent."

In San Antonio after the turn of the century lived a Madam Sckerles, a little German woman in her fifties, who was either psychic or exceedingly clever. San Antonio businessmen swore by her and some would hardly make a policy decision without consulting her first.

On an impulse Webb telephoned Madam Sckerles. Without giving his name, he made an appointment for Tuesday at 3:45. No, she didn't need to know who he was — she would know him when he came.

When he arrived at a small house not far from the heart of downtown San Antonio, he let himself into a plain room where a half-dozen people were waiting. In a moment Madam Sckerles entered, looked about quickly, and said to Webb, "You had the three-forty-five appointment."

In another room she sat him down at a table. He had three things on his mind — should he leave teaching permanently (he had a good business offer), would oil be discovered on his father's property, what sex would his child be? Without prompting on his part, Madam Sckerles looked at him, and said, "I see you surrounded by books. Yes, your life will be with books." She also told him there would be no oil on the family property, and that the child would be a girl.

As Webb stood up to leave, he handed her the fee. She handed half of it back, saying, "For the baby."

She was, of course, correct on all three counts.

While he was still a high school teacher, Walter Webb had appeared on a program of the Texas State Teachers Association. The chairman of a session at which Webb talked about how history should be taught in the public schools was a young medievalist from the University of Texas, Dr. Frederic Duncalf.

Back in Austin, Duncalf conferred with his colleagues. They were generally agreed that the Department of History needed a course for the prospective public school history teacher but none of them cared to leave off his own specialty to tackle the job. Duncalf suggested the high school teacher he had heard in San Antonio. Webb barely had his bachelor's degree, and his grade record was somewhat less than sensational; but he was a University graduate and he did know public school teaching firsthand. At thirty he had had more than a decade of experience.

And so, on Armistice Day, 1918, Walter Prescott Webb, as Madam Sckerles had predicted, moved into a life "surrounded by books." He was still a long way from the goal that the boy "Prescott" had written the *Sunny South* about, but he was at last moving into an environment where people wrote, though few could be classed honestly as writers.

He was also moving insignificantly and at the lowest rank into a school he would serve full time for forty years, a school which would pay him its highest faculty salary, and whose faculty would name him to every elective committee before he retired. When in November, 1958, the University of Texas chose its four most significant living alumni, it named Congressman Sam Rayburn, the record-holding Speaker of the House of Representatives; Robert Anderson, at this writing Secretary of the Treasury; Ramon Beteta, currently Mexico's Minister to Italy; and Walter P. Webb.

One colleague in another department put it this way: "The reason the faculty gave Walter Webb every honor it could bestow was because he never wanted anything."

Perhaps Webb summed it up best when he quoted an old Stephens County philosopher: "Son," the old man had told Webb as a boy, "there's two things you sure as hell don't ever have to tell anybody that you got — brains and money. They'll always find it out sooner or later."

The Great Plains, originally published in 1931, established Walter Prescott Webb, in his mid-forties, as a historian and a writer. It meant more than just a personal triumph. It meant that after three decades he had finally justified the faith of William E. Hinds in an unknown country boy who wanted to write but didn't know where to start.

Several years ago a graduate student asked Webb when he first had begun to study the frontier. "When I was four years old," Webb announced.

His father and mother came out of post-bellum Mississippi. Casner Webb, with a proper Southern view of Yankees, moved into the piney woods of deep East Texas, which is as Southern in outlook, and in some places as much in a time vacuum, as the longleaf country of Mississippi. There Walter Webb had been born on April 3, 1888. Shortly after that, the family moved into the German settlements of South Texas, where they had relatives. Cheap land in quantity had lured Casner P. Webb into the sand and grass and post oaks of Stephens County when his boy was four. There, as Webb said in the preface to his *Great Plains*, "my father and mother gave me a thorough course in Plains life by the direct method, one that enabled me to understand much that I read and to see beyond some of it."

But understanding and liking the life are two different things. A half century later Webb remarked: "It would have been a damned sorry world if it had had to wait on me to make a contribution with my hands. I have no manual dexterity whatsoever. If I'd have had to depend on the skill in my hands, I wouldn't have given the world anything — and the world wouldn't have given me anything either!

"Actually, I never was much use around the farm. By the

time I was ten I was in another world. The farm had completely lost me.

"I tried picking cotton but I never could do anything except make the tips of my fingers sore."

The Great Plains, written with this firsthand knowledge, is so far the most generally successful book Webb has written. When in 1952 the Mississippi Valley Historical Association polled historians for their choices of significant books of the twentieth century, it won a high place, first among those written by living historians. *The Great Plains* triggered men's minds. Fred Shannon of Illinois even wrote a book denouncing Webb's theses, his historical method, and his accuracy. Webb's book, nonetheless, was in 1931 to win the Loubat Prize and be a Book-of-the-Month Club alternate, which it was again in 1936 on republication. It is also understood to have finished second in the 1931 Pulitzer award for history.

The Great Plains appeared just as Webb was leaving to teach a summer session at Duke University. The local newspaper editor — a friend of Webb's, naturally — called him and asked who he would like to review the book. Webb named an Austin journalist, who was also a friend. By the time the review appeared, Webb had reached Durham, where it was forwarded. The first review of his first book, written by a friend, began something like this: "This is a book written largely from secondary materials. It adds nothing to what can be found elsewhere." The remainder of the review dismissed the book as of no importance. Webb was never closer to being heartsick.

And then the next Sunday the *New York Times Book Review* section devoted its front page to *The Great Plains,* calling it "indispensable." Since then, Webb has refused to recommend a reviewer for his books except to tell the inquiring editor, "Just be sure you don't give it to any of my friends!"

After *The Great Plains, The Texas Rangers* appeared, in 1935. Hailed as the definitive history of a frontier law-enforcement agency, it had the faults as well as the virtues of definitiveness. It was overpacked, almost ponderous in its detail; but it hardly left anything for anyone else to say. *The Texas Rangers* had one undoubted advantage. No other book added so much to Webb's memories. The book hit the best-seller lists briefly, and then settled down to an average sale.

Meanwhile, the innumerable expenses that afflict most families had hit Webb's and he was struggling along carefully, his financial head barely above water. He wanted very much to attend the American Historical Association meeting that year, but the budget just wouldn't stretch.

One morning just before Christmas he opened his mail. Paramount Pictures, Inc., was offering him several thousand dollars for the film rights to *The Texas Rangers.*

When Webb attended the American Historical Association meeting the following week, he wore a new suit.

Seventeen years went into the writing of *The Texas Rangers.* Whenever he could, Webb took off time to ride with the Rangers, especially along the one-thousand-mile Rio Grande border. There he studied courage in action, including his own. He came to the conclusion that other men have reached — that fear is no barrier to courage.

Webb took his first trip into the Big Bend with the Rangers in 1923, following the hump-backed dirt and gravel roads over the hills and mountains down to the Rio Grande. He was thrilled by the country; he had never seen anything like it. His company included cowmen as well as Rangers, and the time was not too long after Pancho Villa's raids. His companions were full of lore about each place they came upon.

"You need to see the Big Bend in the company of men who know it for it to mean anything," Webb remarked years later. "With them along, I felt history on me as never before."

He became the close friend of many Rangers. He strapped on a gun and went into the catclaw and *retama* where rode Mexican bootleggers, desperate men seeking a desperate dollar. He drank coffee from a can. He learned to bake biscuits in a Dutch oven. He learned how to live with the prospect of going to bed at night uncertain whether some enemy would permit you to wake in the morning. And he learned to strike out blindly but steadfastly and uncomplainingly for the vaguest of targets, and somehow catch up with the quest. Undoubtedly his Ranger experience helped him develop that thick skin he has exhibited to critics and reviewers. An extremely sensitive, shy man, easily hurt, he can swallow the most stinging criticism of his writings with no visible gulp. As he says often, "Whenever a man publishes, he surrenders his right to be sensitive about the opinions of others."

With the exception of the reply to Fred Shannon, which was requested, and an occasional acknowledgment of factual error, Webb has refused to reply to critics.

The history department at the University of Texas has a history of its own that is perhaps unique among institutions of size. Most of its members entered the department when they were young, and chose to remain. Thus Eugene C. Barker became a member in 1899, and continued until 1951. Charles W. Ramsdell entered the department in 1906; he died in office in 1942. By 1910-12 almost every one of the men with whom Webb taught for three decades was on the staff. There was a stability about the membership that is perhaps unmatched. Webb and Charles W. Hackett, the Latin American historian, were looked on almost as upstarts, since they joined the department as late as 1918.

The department also invariably had one strong man. At first it was George Pierce Garrison, who, as Barker once remarked, "was head of the department and never let you forget it." When Garrison died, Barker was the oldest in point of service and the oldest in age. He was thirty-seven. For forty years he remained the senior member of the department. Never self-assertive, he nonetheless became perhaps the most powerful man on the faculty because of his granite principles. Although there was less than fifteen years' difference in their ages and they served together for three decades, it was rather typical of Webb that he never overcame his diffidence toward Barker, nor ever felt the least familiarity.

"Dr. Barker was the kindest man in the world, but almost fierce in his shyness," Webb observed once. "He could look at me and unnerve me, even though I knew he was kind. If I went into his office with three things on my mind, I would have to make three trips to remember them all!"

In nearly thirty-five years of association, including protracted fishing trips, Webb never once called Barker anything but "Dr. Barker."

When Barker finally stepped down after a career as student and professor that spanned almost sixty years of University of Texas life, Webb took over as bellwether of the history department and of the general faculty.

Like Barker, he rose to the top locally by never seeking to advance himself. Back in the 1930's, when he was still far from secure either professionally or financially, he took his stands quietly and sturdily, with the result that colleagues began to seek him out, even when they disagreed, and University regents began to notice him also.

Twenty years ago the University of Texas established a rank

of Distinguished Professor, to carry an extra stipend above the professorial maximum and to be limited to a dozen men throughout the faculty. When the first appointments were made, Dr. Barker's name was listed, to no one's surprise. Seven years later Charles W. Hackett from the history department was added. Years went by, and although Walter P. Webb was the University's most widely known historian and one of its showpiece professors, he was not tendered the appointment.

Actually, in budget after budget, his name was submitted for the advancement, but, characteristically, Webb had told off a chairman of the Board of Regents, without bothering to blunt his argument, and each time that gentleman persuaded his fellows to veto the University's recommendation of Webb. How long this tug of war might have gone on is uncertain, but when James P. Hart became Chancellor of the University, one of the first things he wanted to know was why Webb was not among the Distinguished Professors. When he learned, he told the regents he considered that this refusal to honor distinction made the rank meaningless, and that the board could take its choice of elevating Webb or finding a new Chancellor. Webb became Distinguished Professor of History.

When apprised of his promotion, Webb gave one of his wry grins. "Honors are funny," he said. "I suspect I deserved this honor a dozen years ago, but I haven't done a damned thing the past ten years to deserve the position, so now I get it!"

On the other hand, the faculty in general cheered the news. And when the story leaked out, as stories always will in an academic group, Chancellor Hart had a faculty which would thenceforward back him almost without question.

And Frank Dobie took time to observe: "One thing sure, Walter Webb has never cowtowed to any power or person in order to advance himself. For him 'A man's a man for a' that' as much as a man was for Robert Burns. He may overestimate an underdog now and then, but Webb'll never be fooled by a stuffed shirt."

And from out of retirement, Dr. Barker wrote that Webb's promotion "was demanded by the undeniably outstanding character of his record."

Although Webb did not publish a major work between 1937 and 1952, he continued to contribute to the cause of history. In 1937-38 he served as consulting historian for the National Park Service. In 1938 he became Harkness Lecturer in American History at the University of London, and during World War II he was Harmsworth Professor of American History at Oxford. He also addressed the International Congress of Historians in Paris in 1950. At various times during his career he collaborated on textbooks with Barker, William E. Dodd, and Henry S. Commager.

In 1937 Webb took another job not designed to promote his own research but charged with service for his region. He became director of the Texas State Historical Association, which publishes the *Southwestern Historical Quarterly*. His administration was notable for several accomplishments. Webb doubled the size of the *Quarterly*, added an unacademic section of odds and ends which he called "Texas Collection," and increased paid advertisements from Texas business institutions. To the annual meeting of the Association, heretofore devoted exclusively to papers, he added a book auction of Texana which attracted collectors from all over the region.

Webb had become convinced that a huge reservoir of youthful interest was going untapped, a reservoir that could feed a steady stream of members and contributors in the decades ahead. The result this time was the creation of the Junior Historian movement among the high school students of the state.

The first five Junior Historian chapters were formed by January, 1940. While there has been no great promotion of other chapters, the total had reached 171 after eighteen years. They have their own statewide magazine, contributed to entirely by their own members. At a conference in New York in 1942 on the Great Plains area, J. Frank Dobie observed the following:

> I don't know but that when Webb gets to St. Peter, he may not have more credit there for the Junior Historians of Texas than he will have for the books he has written, because the far-reachingness, if I may use such a word, of this Junior Historian movement can't be determined at all. . . . I have watched the growing enthusiasm of these young people with great pleasure, and I haven't seen anything in research of a sterner, more formal kind that seems to me at all so important as the spurring on through organization of these people to a realization of their own cultural inheritance, which includes all sorts of history.

Webb also worked out another idea for the Association. In July, 1939, he announced his idea for a thick handbook of Texas, which became a two-volume reality in 1952. Webb saw it as "indispensable to every editor, reporter, library, scholar, and teacher in Texas . . . [and] necessary for every library in the world that made any claim to being a working library." It would be, wrote Webb, "the greatest and most useful piece of scholarship . . . ever issued from this state, and . . . the greatest . . . likely to be done for a long time."

He took his dream to the newspapers. Editorials began to appear. Also critics, who told him that it was too ambitious and too solid for general support. But the University of Texas president at the time, Homer Price Rainey (who, incidentally, stemmed from Webb's bleak Stephens County background), led an attempt to get legislative aid. The result was that the Forty-seventh Legislature appropriated $4750 to survey the project, and subsequent legislatures fell in line. By 1943 the annual budget had hit $12,300 and remained about the same into the 1950's.

The irrepressible Bill Hogan once commented that he was "impressed by Webb's ability to start projects and then escape from the execution of them." *The Handbook of Texas* gives Hogan a case for that statement, for in 1943 Webb stepped down as director of the Association in favor of Dr. H. Bailey Carroll. It was the latter who saw the *Handbook* through to completion, but the promotional hand and the advisory hand of Walter Webb were never very far away. Altogether the *Handbook* had nearly a thousand contributors, paid at encyclopedia rates, who submitted almost 16,000 articles dealing objectively with Texas from prehistory to mid-twentieth century.

In an attempt to raise additional money for the Association, Webb took a turn as an impresario. The Brewers' Association invited Webb to a San Antonio meeting to hear H. G. Wells talk to about a hundred people. Webb wondered whether Wells couldn't draw a large audience in Austin. He learned Wells' fee: $1500.

Webb followed Wells to Dallas, and made him an offer. He would pay Wells $1000. If there were a second $1000 the Association would take that. Anything over $2000 would be split evenly. As the Association had no funds for speakers and Webb had no authorization, he guaranteed the first $1000 out of his own pocket.

Advance sales for the lecture were about $500, and Webb wondered what his loss might be. But the night of the lecture saw cars and buses pour into Austin for the largest non-athletic crowd at Gregory Gymnasium since Will Rogers. At $1 for adults and $.50 for students Webb — or Wells — took in $2700, and everyone was happy.

Over the years the name Walter Prescott Webb has become well known to many Southwesterners who wouldn't — in Webb's words — "walk across the street" to read a book or greet a historian. Invariably the notoriety has come from a sense of service, abetted by an even deeper sense of indignation.

Webb belongs to no service clubs, to no organized pressure groups, to no charitable organizations, and to no church. (Actually, he quietly supports several churches, holds bonds of another, and for a number of years even owned a downtown Lutheran church, which he rented.)

A half-dozen years ago he became indignant because there was no place in downtown Austin where good conversationalists could gather over a long drink or cup of coffee. The taverns were too noisy and commercial, the country clubs too remote, and the Austin Club too expensive and exclusive for many people who were worth listening to. He put his head together with that of Charles Green, editor of the local *American-Statesman*, with the result that the Headliners Club was born. The group is housed in the Driskill Hotel. Dues are modest, as such things go, but its members must all have the ability to make good conversation in the old Samuel Johnson coffeehouse tradition.

Webb belongs to one other social group, this one considerably more fluid, both in membership requirements and activities. Every Thursday night a handful of friends of Joe Small, a young publisher in whose success Webb has had a hand, men in their thirties and forties, gather somewhere for a long session of poker. On an impulse Small asked Webb to join the conclave. It was a mistake, as Webb has been a consistent winner ever since. He plays with the fiendishness of a frontier gambler, and except for a scowl here and there, with the same gambler's poker face.

Small's friends play for relaxation, finesse and money being only incidental — although try telling them that in the middle of a hand! Accordingly, Small was not certain about introducing Webb into the gathering — he was twenty-five years older and they all respected his position and his mind, hardly prerequisites for hilarious camaraderie. Small says that the first two or three games had all the decorum of a woman's missionary society. About the fourth game, however, one of the members bent the rules a bit, and Webb "griped." The offending member looked at Webb's glistening pate, then exploded, "Now, Curly, just take it easy!"

"Dr. Webb," according to Small, "looked at him as if the man had stabbed him with a hot poker — and then gave off with one of his body-shaking guffaws."

Several games later Webb hit a streak of deuces. Every time he stayed in when he felt he shouldn't, he was presented with another deuce for his trouble. Webb became almost violent. Then on one hand, according to Small, "he threw in his cards (after almost deciding to stay) and surely enough, the dealer dropped a deuce on the man to his left. Webb was delighted: 'I fooled that little bastard, didn't I!' "

Despite his lack of sympathy for organizations — and it is no pose — Webb has been honored by a reasonable number of them. In 1953 he was due to be nominated for the vice-presidency of the Mississippi Valley Historical Association and the nominating convention charged me with seeing that he was present — a considerable commission, since he "wouldn't walk across" that street if it looked as if he were seeking honor

To spare you details, he did get to Lexington, grumbling all the way. To make reasonable connections we had to drive two hundred miles to Dallas, fly to Memphis, change planes, de-plane in Louisville, and after a three-hour layover take a bus to Lexington. We left Austin at eight o'clock in the morning, arrived in Lexington at three-thirty the next morning after all the taxis had gone to bed, and wound up walking the last six blocks to the Hotel Phoenix.

As we lugged our bags down the dark streets of Lexington, after 19½ hours on the road, Webb remarked dryly, "Well, this is a fitting end — we've used every known mode of trans-portation except oxcart!"

A year or so before the Lexington convention the American Historical Association met in New York. Webb will always attend conventions in New York, nearly always in Boston and Washington, once in a while in Chicago, and only when he has to anywhere else. He dislikes Chicago because a landlord there once showed him a discourtesy, and he will never be able quite to forgive the city. But New York fascinates him.

A half-dozen members from the University's department at-tended this particular annual meeting. After we had returned, a departmental luncheon was held at which Lewis Hanke sug-gested that each tell what sessions he had attended and what of significance or interest he had heard. Each gave his account of several sessions, until finally it was Webb's turn.

"Oh hell, Hanke," he said. "I took one look at the program and then went to see *Guys and Dolls* and *The Consul* and I don't know what else. I can listen to historians any time!"

Webb is a Texan, quite happy in Texas, but once he crosses the Red River boundary, he feels that he has been turned loose in the world. No matter where any out-of-state convention is held, he will always come home by way of New York. At the Lexington convention, for instance, we had round-trip tickets, but on the last day of the convention he said, "Let's go on to New York and Washington, Joe, we're so close."

Whenever Webb does go on a trip he is likely to be gone twice to three times as long as he planned. Several years ago I went with him to Kingsville, about 200 miles from Austin, for a commencement address. Three hours after we left we had reached San Marcos, 32 miles to the south. By nightfall we had reached San Antonio, 80 miles along the route. He knows people in every town and he likes to call some old friend, seldom an academic, who will call six others. The first thing you know, there is a small mob at some local coffee shop, talking and listening.

He finished his stint at Kingsville, looked at me, grinned slyly, and said, "Have you ever met Vann Kennedy?"

I hadn't, although I knew Kennedy was a former Austin newspaperman and political maneuverer who now ran a radio station in Corpus Christi. We spent one afternoon with him in the Nueces Hotel coffee shop, absorbing impressions of politics in South Texas and listening to realtors and more-or-less literati and tavern owners tell us what made Corpus grow.

That night we spent in the Denver Hotel in Victoria, because I had never seen the furniture — all antiques — and besides, the owner was a former state senator whom Webb thought was "precious." The following night we spent in Galveston, because he had never been to the Balinese Room, and for no discernible reason he wanted to go with a younger companion.

Five nights later we showed up in Austin. We had a view of the Texas littoral from just about every angle and from just about every occupational group. Although comparisons are odious, one can't escape the feeling that Webb would have loved to be a journalist of the John Gunther stripe, and that he would have been as successful in nosing about and absorbing what he saw as he has been in the historical profession. He is constantly, though not vocally, annoyed at his colleagues, who stick to their halls of ivy (which in Texas is strictly a euphemism!).

"Why, I bet —— doesn't go to town once a year except to buy shoes!" he said recently of a colleague. As for Webb, he can almost always be found somewhere — at his typewriter in Garrison Hall, but just as likely visiting the busboy at the Night Hawk or drinking coffee at the Headliners late at night. He goes everywhere alone, but because he is known by so many people around Austin he never winds up alone.

Meanwhile he is sought out by students for personal charities, by Mexicans needing work, by men in trouble with their wives, and by bankers needing advice on real estate loans. His success at spotting population trends has made him locally fabled, as well as financially prosperous, so that his telephone jangles regularly, with someone on the other end having lined up a "sure thing" for him to invest in. He has accomplished the feat of becoming a major property holder in Austin with only a professor's salary to work with by being constantly in debt. The only times he has missed have been when he was timid and refused to extend his debt load. Austin and Houston businessmen who know him will tell you that if he had chosen to pursue money-making as a full-time career instead of just a means of piecing out his salary, his name would have been included among Texas' storied "Big Rich" of whom the slick magazines make so much. That, of course, is guessing, but there is no arguing with his ownership of apartment houses, churches, taverns, rent houses, commercial properties, and a ranch.

In his real estate dealings it is hard to tell when Webb is showing hardheaded farm-boy common sense and when emotion or intuition takes over. The ranch is a case in point. He purchased the ranch when he couldn't afford it, because a local realtor persuaded him that the drive eighteen miles out in the country couldn't possibly hurt him.

As the owner of a ranch — mostly cedar brakes and no grass — Webb wondered what to do next. He tried running Santa Gertrudis cattle and spent — wasted, in his words — several years that should have been put in on research. Then the idea hit of making a summer camp of it — a camp that would have facilities but would in the main be a bit on the rugged side. So he sank money in a swimming pool, persuaded the highway department to dam up a small creek that ran — when it ran — through the property, concreted a tennis court, and went into the boys' camp business at prices stiff enough that only the wealthier could afford it. Instead of horses, he stocked it with donkeys.

Friday Mountain Camp was an instantaneous and continuing success, with a clientele from all over the Southwest and a waiting list. Webb sees it as a creation — he hires drag lines to remake hills, and he brings out soil and grass experts to try out new cover; but he also sees it for what it is, another money-making venture.

"Depressions may come and most of us may have to tighten our belts," he observes, "but I figure there'll always be a River Oaks section with enough money to be snobbish."

The ranch also gives Webb a place to throw a party every year or two. He personally types out about two dozen invitations, oversees the cooking, furnishes everything, and in general has a party that makes those invited willing to drive in from several hundred miles away. The invitations themselves are written with obvious relish. His latest included his guest list, as follows:

The Guests: Authors, editors, publishers, and such sages as Bill Kittrell [a leading Texas politician]. Denizens of Houston, Dallas, San Antonio, San Marcos, Circleville,

Cedar Valley, and New York. There will be singers, pic-
colo players, naturalists, columnists, liars, entertainers,
Saturday Evening cowboys, and other primitive artists.
About twenty men, noted for bias, prejudice and opinions,
characteristics which appear after moderate applications
of Bear Creek Branch Water. The man who holds the
floor for three minutes without being interrupted and
contradicted will deserve a prize.

You are Invited because it is believed that you will add
to the fun and confusion.

There was also a note: "The fastidious might bring a bar of
soap."

Webb and Roy Bedichek agreed once to ward off old age by
committing one foolish act a year. Webb has pretty well lived
up to that agreement. One day he hailed me on the campus.

"I've done my fool stunt for this year!" He grinned.

"What is it?"

He explained. A group of workmen were tearing down an
old shack in the more raffish part of East Austin. When they
ripped off the beer signs and then the tar paper underneath,
they discovered a log cabin. Someone called Webb, who, having ascertained that the cabin had been around for several
generations, bought it on the spot, called in an architect's
assistant and master carpenters, and spent hours overseeing the
dismantling and numbering of the logs. The cabin was then
moved to his ranch and reassembled. It must have cost him
the price of a small house.

"Now what in hell do I want with a log cabin!" He thought
a minute, then shrugged. "Anyway, I've got one."

Later, in the summer of 1955, Webb wrote me as follows:

Since you have left I have bought a new car, Plymoth,
and another log cabin. I can't spell Plymouth, but I can

spell cabin. The car was reasonable but the cabin was outrageous. It's the most magnificent deluxe model that I have seen, two doors, one unstreamlined window, an unairconditioned attic with hand-tooled logs and no toilet. The cracks let in the mice, but keep out the possums and skunks. The front door has a cat hole, and in case you never heard of that, it is a place where the cat can excuse himself without embarrassing himself by asking some favor of a human being for whom he has such contempt. I guess the poor devoted dog had to sleep on the porch. A family of ten children grew up in the cabin at one time, whch shows that it must not have been a bad place to be on long rainy nights. Under present ownership, the cabin will look back with nostalgia on the good old days. No analogies please!

One characteristic that Webb has in common with the traditional Texan is his disregard for distance. Especially if there is good talk promised. In New York once, he called a Boston editor to say that he was flying up for the day just to talk with him. The editor, not a native Bostonian and therefore overproper, discouraged Webb's coming, as he had a tea date out in Cambridge.

"Hell," snorted Webb, "he treated Cambridge like it was a three-days' trip!"

One of his favorite talkers is Fred Gipson, the novelist and creator of such characters, human and animal, as "Hound-Dog Man" and "Old Yeller." Gipson lives on a small ranch outside Mason, 110 miles northwest of Austin.

"A couple of years ago," Gipson recalls, "Walter called me from Austin. In the voice of a little boy about to sneak off and throw rocks at telephone-line insulators, he wanted to know, 'Fred, have you got any whiskey on hand?'

"I told him to come up, that I possibly could supply enough;

so he drove to Mason, spent five hours, talking grass, boyhood days, the water problem, politics, etc., and consuming at least a couple of fingers of bourbon, then left for Austin, apparently satisfied that the afternoon had been well spent."

There is no counting the trips that Webb has made to Houston, 160 miles in another direction, just to listen to talk by George Fuermann, the biographer of *Reluctant Empire: The Mind of Texas*. When one less mobile acquaintance asked Webb why he would drive 320 miles just to visit for a couple of hours, he replied, almost with surprise, "Why, George is civilized!"

William E. Hinds' generous gamble on young Walter P. Webb has left its beneficiary something of a soft touch for students. Webb's office in Garrison Hall is conveniently near to a pay telephone. Since he works most of the time with his door open, students are forever interrupting to borrow nickels to make calls. Most of them he has never seen before; those who know him tend, with a few impertinent exceptions, to be a little afraid of his gruff manner. So far as he knows, he has never turned down a request or lost a nickel — the student is always back in a day or two.

His charities go far beyond the nickel-and-dime stage, however. When several years ago a young history instructor was having housing difficulties, complicated by personal financial straits, Webb and Barker bought the man a house so that he wouldn't have to worry about finances when he was supposed to be starting a career. (Incidentally, the young man responded by moving to a better job the following fall. Webb finds the episode a little funny.)

No one knows how many students he has put through school. Or helped set up in business.

John Haller was a tall mustached student majoring in English, who wandered into one of Webb's seminars. A restless sort, Haller began to spend whatever spare time he had from a master's thesis on Mark Twain's *Joan of Arc* trimming trees around Austin. He tells his own story.

"Soon I found that we needed a truck, but this being during the war years, trucks were hard to come by. Dr. Webb said that he had one he was not using, whereupon I asked if he would sell or rent it to me.

" 'I don't want to sell it, and I won't rent it to you,' Webb said, 'but I'll let you use it as long as you want to.'

" 'Are you keeping busy?' he asked me one day about six months later.

" 'I'm starving to death,' I answered modestly.

"The next morning he had me and my crew out on his Friday Mountain ranch, going over the trees.

" 'Work here until business in town picks up,' he said. 'Don't hurry to get through.' "

On one other occasion Haller had a problem, this time needing an apartment when they were virtually impossible to find. He went to Webb.

"He took me in his car," writes Haller, "to a place on the outskirts of the city, where a small frame house stood vacant.

" 'It needs a little fixing up,' he said. 'But if you want it, you can live there until you find something better.'

" 'How much is the rent?' I asked.

" 'Nothing,' he answered. 'How do you think I can charge you? You are just beginning. I've already lived my life.' "

Once Webb told J. Frank Dobie that before he dies he wants to leave a visible mark to honor William E. Hinds.

"Men who keep gratitude in their hearts for a lifetime," observes Dobie, "and want to pay inner debts that nobody else knows about do not run in herds."

Webb did once publicly pay his respects to Hinds. The dedication of *The Texas Rangers* reads as follows: "To the memory of William Ellery Hinds. He fitted the arrow to the bow, set the mark, and insisted that the aim be true. His greatness is best known to me."

While Haller was working at Friday Mountain, "an amiable, leisurely moving old codger" came out of the ranch house several times a day to visit. The caretaker, thought Haller — or a pensioner. Except that his conversation was so wide-ranging, and he seemed to know every bird on the place.

The "amiable old codger" was Roy Bedichek, not exactly a youth, and definitely not the caretaker. He directed the University's Interscholastic League, but was better known among his cronies as the man who could make the best talk they had ever heard. Men like Webb and J. Frank Dobie would gladly drop whatever project they were buried in to listen to Bedichek.

Webb thought about Bedichek. What a waste to let this man's erudition and gift of expression die with his mortal body. But like so many other academics, especially those with administrative duties, Bedichek was so buried in details that he could never get the stretching room necessary to write anything except of the most transient character.

With Dobie, Webb got in touch with other men who revered Bedichek. The result was that ten of them put up $500 apiece and persuaded Bedichek to retire for a year to Webb's ranch, not to emerge till he had a book completed. Webb felt that Mrs. Bedichek looked a bit askance at this interruption to their *modus operandi*, but the results have again justified the investment.

Bedichek started writing when he was pushing seventy years of age. Now nearly eighty, he has published three books, which have won for him an international reputation as a field naturalist and philosopher. Two of them have received major prizes. He ranks with Dobie as the only man to have won the

Texas Institute of Letters Award more than once. And all of this after seventy.

In 1953 Webb made a speech in Dallas in which he urged the Texas wealthy to take a page from his life and underwrite an investment in youth, particularly in the type of youth who burns to write but who wears himself out in the battle for subsistence. Webb's own investment has gone far beyond youth. This past year he took out three months to help an amateur put together a manuscript about her experiences with a husband who was a professional fisherman. The cost in time and trips to the Gulf coast may never be repaid, but Webb would rather see the would-be author realize a dream than get on with his own career.

At least four times Webb has jumped in over his head. In none of these instances was he guilty of his deliberate, once-a-year foolishness, but instead he jumped for indignation and then found he couldn't turn back.

In the middle 1930's the federal government and the state of Texas seemed to Webb to be idling their motors with regard to the establishment of the Big Bend National Park, a real left-over of frontier days. Webb had seen this country in his Texas Ranger days and looked on it as romantic and unspoiled. He decided to force the hand of the Texas legislature then in session.

With a handful of Rangers, game wardens, and the like, Webb set out to traverse the Santa Elena canyon of the Rio Grande. This trip had been made before, but, as the Dallas *News* pointed out, the canyon's floor had been seen by fewer white men than either of the polar regions. The voyage was a newspaperman's natural, so that a good portion of the state watched the intrepid — or fool — historian try to run the gantlet of rapids, whirlpools, and who knew what else.

Later Webb confessed he didn't feel at all intrepid, but more like a man gone daft. He couldn't understand why he had planned the trip, but having made the decision he could hardly back out. And so on May 16, 1937, he entered the upper end of the canyon, wondering whether he would ever see the lower. He did, and has lived almost a quarter century since.

Whether Webb's "stunt," for essentially that is what it was, influenced any legislative and executive bodies is impossible to know, but the fact is that both the federal and state agencies came through and every year Big Bend National Park attracts more tourists to its remote, raw beauties.

The second plunge came on the night that Webb heard of the United States Supreme Court's having thrown out the National Recovery Administration. Angered and a little sick, he sat down to his typewriter and began work on a book of protest. *Divided We Stand* annoyed more people than it pleased, and Webb's original publishers withdrew the book from circulation because its chapter on Hartford Empire Glass offended persons in high places. But the book has stayed in print, one way or another, and has continued to annoy for two decades now.

Webb, having grown up in country that was — and is — basically barren, watched his father fight a water problem. As a ranchman himself, he watched his grass dry away, and sold his cattle because the rains refused to come. Seven years of drought came to Texas, beginning at the end of the 1940's. The people, especially their elected representatives, complained about the falling water table and the succession of crop failures, but their efforts at relief were, in Webb's eyes, timid and tentative.

"Not oil, not gas, but water is our most critical natural resource," he liked to say. Although his colleagues in economics and in business administration disagreed with him, he was convinced that until Texas solved the water problem, it would never approach its potential. He began to sound off at the coffee table. Before long, he was being asked to speak at meetings of various types of people concerned with water. Texas is a large state, and he would drive 700 miles round trip, often with not even expenses paid, because some group wanted to hear what he had to say about the water problem in Texas. He wrote articles for magazines. When the Bureau of Reclamation submitted a report on the Texas water situation, Webb decided that the report needed to be more widely read than the usual government document.

Accordingly, he brought out a small book, *More Water for Texas*, putting the Bureau's ideas into layman's language. The Eisenhower administration sent for him to come to Washington to be honored. He went — at his own expense. How much he accomplished in his lonely way is again difficult to assay, for he worked without organization, a sort of water missionary preaching in the wilderness. What the cost to him was in time taken from his historical studies, and what the cost was in money are also unascertainable.

On the other hand, in the 1956 Texas gubernatorial campaign every major candidate took a definite stand for a program of water conservation. It was one of the two or three major issues. The Texas legislature passed new water measures, not as expensive and sweeping as Webb was urging, but still representing considerable progress in a government that tends to be more interested in economy than in expansion.

The fourth plunge concerns the article he wrote for *Harper*'s entitled "The American West: Perpetual Mirage." Webb had read a book of Lucius Beebe's on the West and had found it as synthetic as Las Vegas. He wrote a review that grew into an essay of a dozen pages. Webb's desk itself is a magnificent disarray, and books and unopened packages, ox yokes and letters that haven't been disturbed in months, litter his office; in this confusion he promptly lost the review. Not willing to repeat immediately the research that went into salving his pique, he wrote a regulation-size, regulation-tempered review, but couldn't forget the artificiality that he thought went into Beebe's book.

He renewed his study of the West, and came up with the idea that the distinguishing feature of Western history is that there is so little of it, and that the reason there is so little history is that the region is too nearly a desert, geographically, politically, culturally, and historically.

When he submitted the article to *Harper*'s, its editors were delighted. So were its salesmen, who saw that every Western governor, congressman, and Chamber of Commerce secretary was made aware of Webb's charges. The mail came from all over, a positive deluge — or gully-washer — to keep the Western figure. The Dallas *News*, concerned with its city's need to market bonds in the Eastern marts, hit Webb with four articles and editorials in one issue. The anger was just as intense and just as sincere in Tucson and in Helena. The Denver *Post* talked to him long-distance for nearly an hour. The only good responses came from the rainbelts.

With a mountain of fan mail, if it could be called that, Webb had the time of his life. The gist of many of the letters was that Webb should go back where he came from, the implication being that he was some marsh-Yankee who had inadvertently wandered into a man's land, and couldn't take it.

When subsequently Webb reviewed Edmund C. Jaeger's *The North American Deserts*, he pointed out almost gleefully that the book, while excellent, would receive little attention and raise no hackles, even though it utilized scientific findings to support his thesis that the West had an oasis civilization.

"People do not mind what a biologist has to say about the influence of the desert on plants and animals," he wrote, "but some mind very much if a historian points out that the desert has a comparable influence on the human animal."

J. Frank Dobie and Walter Prescott Webb are almost exactly the same age. They tend to attract the same bands of admirers, though Dobie stirs a strong devotion from the feminine contingent, both in groups and individually, which Webb does not; they also attract the same bands of detractors. Their careers are closely intertwined with the University of Texas, they both are fiercely independent, they both have annoyed the University's Boards of Regents, and they are idolized by their students, with the usual strong-minded, rebellious exceptions.

Their works are, of course, most frequently identified with the Southwest of their origin; and yet they both have moved far beyond mere regionalism. To many Texans and non-Texans alike, they are the typical Texans, though neither is tall or thin-shanked or inclined to loud boasting or is parochial in outlook. Often they are lumped together as Western writers. This assertion — or charge — is dead wrong. To Harry Ransom, Dobie looks like Robert Frost or Carl Sandburg, and his thinking is influenced more by Socrates and Plato and his writing by John Milton than by anything or anybody Texan.

What Ransom says of Dobie holds for Webb also. Take away his expensive, grease-stained Stetson, and Webb could look like any Middletown, U.S.A., banker. Of medium height and medium weight, wearing a suit that is tailor-made and high-priced, he shambles along as if he were walking plowed ground, his tie a little crooked and not quite two-blocked, looking neither to left nor right. Unlike Dobie, who is extremely "pettable," Webb grunts greetings, if he sees you at

all. He has affronted more than one person, and he is no good
at all at small talk. If he has nothing to say, he says nothing.

Between Webb and Dobie exists a sort of armed affection.
Each respects the other, but each, their friends believe, is just
a mite jealous.

"Webb is one historian who never lets the evidence stand
in the way of the truth — as he sees it," said Dobie, introducing Webb at a Dallas dinner.

"Frank can sell the same story to more different magazines
than anyone I've ever seen," Webb has charged.

But underneath, the generosity of each toward the other is
real.

Once, Dobie recalls, Webb said to him, "Many times I wish
I did not have to think."

"As for me," observes Dobie, "until recent years, thinking
has been an unnatural process. Consequently, I have regarded
thinkers as something almost curious. Walter Webb is the
most powerful thinker I have known. I mean that he, more
than anybody else I know, wrings meanings out of facts. He
is the very opposite of the quiz-kid experts and the know-how
factotums. Clem Yore, one of the old-time producers of Western fiction who tried to be authentic, wrote me that he and
some other Western writers didn't know what barbed wire and
windmills meant until they read *The Great Plains*."

Dobie continues. "I've known Webb since he came to the
University forty years ago. Lately I've been noticing how
much more flexible and limber he is in his intellectual move-
ments than he was when his knees were more limber. That's
because he has exercised his head more than his knees. He has
entered into that supreme joy of a man's maturest years — a
state that has drawbacks terrifying to the merely physical — the
joy of having a free and liberated mind, totally unrestricted by
superstitions of party, economics, religion, or anything else.
He loves to sit on what Dr. Johnson called 'the throne of hu-

man felicity' and enjoy play of mind and to tell stories and warm his innards at the fire of comradeship."

The death of Charles W. Hackett in 1951 depressed Webb terribly. For one thing, he and Webb were the same age and had entered University employment about the same time. Other men in the history department had died, but they had been older. At the funeral Webb had looked around, and suddenly the men he had known and accepted as young men and the wives he had known as pretty, ambitious young girls had aged thirty years. He felt a strong desire to flee the church.

On the way out a colleague in his fifties hailed Webb and suggested coffee.

"No!" Webb answered curtly. "I want to be with young people."

My wife and I were the nearest things to young people anywhere about, and we sat with him in a booth at the Night Hawk for two hours. But we had an engagement that couldn't be broken, and we left him.

Webb then looked up Dobie, who is not exactly a youth. They bought some crackers and cheese and drove to Webb's ranch. It was February, and only the two of them were in the silent stone house. They sat past midnight, sometimes quiet, sometimes reminiscing, moving only to slice more cheese.

It was friendship at its fullest.

Dobie expressed it simply when he wrote: "There's an old Western saying: 'He'll do to ride the river with.' Walter Webb will do to ride the river with until the water all dries up."

Since Walter Webb is not athletic, is seldom impetuous, does not play practical jokes, and dislikes sophistry, he is not a man who surrounds himself with anecdotes. What delights his friends and insults others is his pithiness of speech — pithiness

with now and then a touch of strong brine. He has an ability
to see through a complex problem and to dispose of it with a
sentence. He has the gift and the fault of oversimplification
that traditionally is reserved for barbers and bus drivers, but
never for academics, who see too many facets and qualify the
life out of answers.

Texas had seven searing, withering years of drought. In the
spring of 1956 it began to rain beyond all memory, and continued into the spring of 1957. As Webb and I drove to
Houston this past May, the grass was waist-high in the fields,
wild flowers spread their blues and yellows and reds to the
horizon, and tanks were filled to the brim with water. It didn't
look at all like the brown, bare Texas we all had suffered for
so long. Webb gazed about.

"You know," he said, "this is the year we should sell the
whole state of Texas to some damned Yankee and get out
while we're ahead!"

On another day he was idling across the campus with Frank
Wardlaw, director of the University of Texas Press, when a
colleague crossed their path.

"Damned academic armadillo!" Webb muttered.

"What did you say?" asked Wardlaw.

"I said the man's an academic armadillo," Webb said
testily.

"What do you mean?"

"He's got a shell so thick no idea could possibly penetrate it,
and he pokes his anteater's nose into everything."

When the tables are turned on Webb, he loves it as much
as anyone else, especially if the remark has come from an
elevator operator, or waitress, or laborer, and tends to set
arrogance at rest.

An Austin man encountered a Negro downtown. "You
work for Dr. Webb, don't you?" he asked the Negro.

"No suh," the Negro answered. "Dr. Webb, he works for me!"

"And you know," Webb said later, "the more I thought of it, the more I decided he was right — I've got to keep working to afford him!"

One of Webb's more frequent quotations is that of the age-less Negro baseball pitcher, Satchel Paige, "Don't look back, somethin' might be gainin' on yuh!" One suspects that Webb likes the quotation because it emanated from Paige, and that if it had come from the lips of some M.P. during parliamentary debate, he would have found it neither memorable nor humorous.

In Hillsboro, Texas, is the Andrews Café, a pretty good restaurant with the usual small-town limitations. Webb and his family were returning from his mother's funeral in two cars, when they stopped for coffee at the Andrews. Webb went in ahead of the second car, and unthinkingly gave his order. He must have been short with the waiter; he can be very short.

In a moment the second carload entered, sat at another table, and waved to Webb. The waiter went to their table, took the orders, and then said, "Who is that man and what does he do?"

"His name is Walter Webb, and he teaches at the University."

"Well," said the waiter, "he may be the smartest man in the country, but he sure as hell could stand to learn some manners!"

One of the party told Webb, who promptly went over to the waiter, apologized, and talked with him at some length. Now Webb and Skip Middleton, the waiter, are old friends, and Webb never goes through Hillsboro without stopping to get insulted.

Professor Bert Barksdale of Arlington State College in Texas

was with Webb and a group who were condemning an individual whose philosophy in every respect was opposed to
Webb's.

Finally, Webb broke in. "Well, he's all right. He can bake
the best biscuits ever eaten on the range."

Barksdale also attended a meeting at which Webb read a
paper. Most of his papers provoke comment and heated criticism, and this one was no exception. Some of the criticisms
hit hard, and undoubtedly stung. Finally, the chairman asked
whether Webb had any answer to the carping crescendo.

"He stalked to the center of the platform," recalls Barksdale,
"gazed over the crowd, split his sour face with his matchless
grin, and said, 'I agree with everything my distinguished critics
have said.' "

From the audience: no more comment.

When Frank Dobie remarked that Webb could see meanings behind facts, Webb retorted that the reason he saw meanings was because he had to.

"I never could remember facts," he said. "Why, I never sat
in on a student's doctoral examination that I could have
passed!"

Webb is steeped enough in O. Henry to like to pull a last-
minute straight-faced stinger. When Wardlaw assumed di-
rectorship of the University of Texas Press, he asked Webb for
an ecstatic comment concerning his first publication, *The
Florida of the Inca.* After considerable grumbling, Webb com-
plied.

> Though I have read many accounts of Spanish explora-
> tion in America, I can recall none which has the charm,
> grace of expression, and simplicity that I find in Gar-
> cilaso's story. He had that rare ability to write in such a
> manner as to present a series of graphic pictures which

stand in clear outline before the mind of the reader. It is
this gift that drives the reader along through page after
page of the narrative, and that should give this book an
audience much bigger than that composed of scholars
and research students. The story is perfectly fascinating,
and I shall probably have to read it.

On another occasion a group of us were talking about a
pioneer Austin cattlewoman, now dead. This one described
her and that one described her, and then Webb walked up.
We told him whom we were talking about.

"Her!" Webb exclaimed. "Why, she was so mean she had
to climb upstairs to get in Hell!"

A historian in another state has a brother in West Texas.
Learning this, Webb looked him up and disliked him on sight.

"Why?" I asked.

"Because he's a stuffed shirt, the type who even struts sitting down!"

Although he would be the last to hand out free advice,
Webb is constantly making suggestions that he insists his audi-
tors not take seriously. Not at all pontifical, he feels that
neither position nor age gives him or anyone else insight into
another man's problems. If you go to him for help, he will listen, try to help you see your alternatives clearly, and then say,
"But do what you want to do — it's the only way you'll be
happy."

When I spent the summer of 1956 in New York, I wrote
him about a work problem. He replied: "Go to all the good
shows you can. Memory of them outlasts all else."

Much of his advice is really directed at himself. In that
same summer of 1956 he spent several days in Montana with
such Western fiction writers as A. B. Guthrie, Norman Fox,

and Walter Van Tilburg Clark. He was impressed with their output.

"My point is," he wrote a colleague, "that we sit on our tails in Texas and swell up to inordinate size if we write one book. What we need to do is to shed an inferiority complex, tighten our belts, and make the most of what we've got. What has happened to me, and it happens when I get away to New York or to the West, is that I am all swollen with a sense of power and good resolutions, which, when I get back to Texas, will dissolve in sweat and run down my left leg. It's hell to be lazy and ambitious at the same time. Of course in my case time is running out, but this morning I don't realize it, which means I feel young and good."

He was once telling a colleague how he "peddled" *The Texas Rangers*. He first saw the Little, Brown editor, who said he liked what he had seen of the manuscript, would take it, and would pay $500 in advance. Webb gathered his manuscript off the table and prepared to leave.

"You're going to let us have it, aren't you?" asked the editor.

"Frankly, I'm shopping. I will sell this manuscript only once. I may let you have it, but I want to look around first for the best offer."

He walked over to Houghton Mifflin Company, where he saw Ferris Greenslet and warmed up to him immediately. Greenslet said, "I like the manuscript. We'll pay you $1000 now, $1000 on receipt of the completed manuscript, and another $1000 on the day of publication." He also promised to spend $2500 in advertising.

"As I went outside," Webb recalls, "I had to kick a few stars out of my way, I was riding so high. They had $5500 invested in me — I knew they'd work hard to get their money out."

In a faculty or departmental gathering Webb tends to stay quiet, almost indifferent, until finally the inaction brought on by argument nettles him. Then he pitches in, quickly, incisively, and usually sees the problem settled. At the University of Texas six hours of American history is required by law of all graduates. This means that about 2500 students take the sophomore survey each semester. The course is taught by 25 to 40 faculty and teaching assistants, and involves most of the department. We were having a departmental meeting at which I had raised a question that was debated for an hour, and Webb was poring over a term paper, seemingly not listening. Suddenly he looked up and said, "It's Joe's course — why not let him go ahead and do what he wants!" Although it definitely was not *my* course, his remark so shocked the department that action was taken immediately.

The next day Webb stopped me in the hall with that ineffable grin on his face.

"Sort of surprised them yesterday, didn't I?" he said. "I tell you, Joe, I've found that those who accomplish anything never waited for committees or authority or anything, but went ahead and did what needed doing. I'm as democratic as the next person — more democratic than most. But if you wait for a group to decide something, you'll still be waiting a month from now."

When a colleague was offered a position away from the University, Webb wrote him:

The offer is attractive, and I am not saying that you should resist the attraction. You are for several reasons going to be presented with many lures and many opportunities. This fact places heavy responsibility on you as to the choices you make and increases your chances of making some wrong choices. At a certain stage of development, you must know what to refuse and must be resolute in refusing. If not, you are soon under more obligations than you can fulfill, and that is extremely bad for that spiritual repose in which the best work is done. The solution is to formulate your own program, cut out a job that you really want to do and that is important enough to you to make those other lures easy to decline. A cowboy with sex appeal, one of Badger Clark's characters, solved the problem by marrying one girl and letting her stand off all the others.

Some scholars are pilgrims who have a fixed destination, others are hoboes who will go anywhere that a convenient train runs. The men who have made reputations in scholarship have been pilgrims rather than hoboes, though I suspect that the hoboes may have had more variety and perhaps more fun. I am moved to repeat this lecture because your name comes up so often here when there is a new job to do. "Good ole Mack — he can do anything." Maybe, but he can't do everything.

When a companion began to feel his importance, Webb decided to bring him gently back to earth: "Whenever I get to feeling like I'm somebody — and I recommend this for any University man who gets to feeling like a big-shot bastard — I go to San Antonio and stand on that busy corner outside the Gunter Hotel for an hour and just watch the people go by and ask myself how many of all those persons ever heard of Walter Webb or ever gave one thought to the University of Texas in a day's time, or even cared whether the University exists or goes to hell. That puts things back in perspective."

Eventually John Haller, the graduate student in English turned tree surgeon, wrote a book on trees. He looked up Webb for advice.

Webb commented, "Why should you care for my opinion? The only critic whose opinion matters is the publisher."

When Haller had his contract, he went back to talk to

Webb about sales prospects. Again, Webb told him that any money he made would be incidental to the fact that his book was published.

"But what about the seven years I've spent working on this thing?" Haller protested. "I would have been better off in a barroom."

"That's not the way to look at it," Webb answered quietly. "You are now an authority on the subject. You will be asked to speak here and there, and the book will bring you new friends and new contacts. The royalty checks don't tell the whole story. There are by-products in books as well as in beef."

Around the University campus Walter Webb's almost intuitive seeking out of people who need help is a legend. Bluff and apparently hard-boiled and unapproachable, he nonetheless senses needs in other people.

Perhaps the most remarkable facet of Webb's helpfulness — indeed, of his whole influence — lies in the fact that he operates perpendicularly rather than horizontally. Many academicians inspire a following in their particular age, rank, or departmental layers; but at the University Webb crosses all lines with ease. No perennial Young Man, he nonetheless deals easily with youth. An older member of the faculty, he also avoids identification with what Vice-President Ransom calls "the Golden Years Club."

"This is important," insists Ransom, "for the continuity of University tradition has often been disturbed or defeated by the failure of one generation to talk easily and honestly with others. Webb savvies all kinds of academic brutes, including even administrators."

One of the younger members of the faculty had aroused an intense dislike among some of his seniors. The antipathy, it might be added, was mutual. One day Webb, who ordinarily wouldn't speak fifteen sentences in a year to the young man, hailed him as he was leaving the campus. He asked him whether he had a half-hour for some coffee; they wound up riding the thirty-six miles to the ranch and back, tramping over the countryside, and mainly just talking. Although the young man's trouble was never mentioned, his attitude cleared, for he knew that somehow he had found an older friend who would see him through if it ever became necessary.

The Dean of Arts and Sciences at the University is J. Alton Burdine, a man about fifty. In 1936, when he was brand-new to the University, he and a group of other academic newcomers were named to a committee to plot the future of the University. Oddly, the President picked all young men for the committee, on the thesis that it would be they, and not the established stars, who would have to teach in the University of two decades thence. When the young committee brought in its report the next year, some of the older faculty launched — in faculty meeting — a well-executed belittling attack, pointing up the inexperience and starry-eyed qualities of the committee. Burdine, as chairman of the committee, felt crushed.

A week later, still depressed, he was walking past the Austin National Bank when he heard his name called. "Burdine!"

He turned around. It was Webb, whom he had never met. But the mere fact that Webb knew his name inspirited him. There followed the usual long cup of coffee, during which Webb told him dispassionately what was good and what was bad about the committee report. Burdine has come to Webb with many academic problems since.

School boards, superintendents, principals, and presidents have studied for years the problem of how to evaluate teachers fairly. The problem is still being wrestled with, and the solution seems no nearer.

How then do you assess Walter Webb as a teacher? You can point out that he communicates a love of reading and writing; that he brings a universality of interest; that he has a sense of appropriateness to his crowd; that he intrigues his students because he vacillates between being extremely gregarious and just as lone-wolfish; and that he throws out thoughts. He is not the polished lecturer, and is especially given to starting sentences that he never finishes, just as he starts projects that he walks off and leaves.

Webb has the classroom ability of stirring his students. Many of the brighter ones, especially if they come from such other disciplines as economics and philosophy, enter his class determined to prove that his interpretations are too scattergun to stand up. Not infrequently they come away still unconvinced that he has any contribution to make in the world of ideas, but in reaching that lack of conviction they have delved widely and deeply. Webb, of course, doesn't care whether they agree. He is merely interested in stimulating them to ideas.

The more violent they are in disagreeing with Webb the more likely they are to come up with an A in his course, for he would never want a student to think he was vindictive or dogmatic. Besides, he is a rather high grader, despite the fact that he can lose patience with illogical argument.

His seminars, invariably held at night, are famous, and no graduate student in history would think of winding up his University of Texas career without exposing himself to one of them. He gives the students problems and then sits back to see where the research falls. He encourages class criticism, but has no sympathy whatever for the tendency among academic groups to go beyond what he calls "gentlemanly behavior" in their critiques.

On the other hand, if a student is trying to be glib where he should be full of knowledge, Webb will set him down in a hurry. He has never had patience with anyone, student or colleague, who had nothing to say. On several occasions he has startled University deans and even presidents by putting on his hat and walking out in the middle of a sentence. He wasn't being rude. It was just that he had finished what he had come for, and so he left.

"Discussion can never proceed without disagreement," he has said, "and that is all to the good, and a university campus is the best forum for such disagreement as long as the views expressed are reasonable and to the point.

"Interpretations and interpreters are fallible because the interpreter is a fallible human being. But no interpretation has ever had universal acceptance, and none should. It is those who differ who correct history and keep the subject alive.

"An interpretation has another value in that it gives to those who accept it a frame of reference, a place to take off from and to come back to in trying to understand the past."

And so he goes on in class, reading Joaquin Miller and Gene Rhodes and even Damon Runyon to make his points, or mixing in Ortega y Gasset and Carl Becker on another level.

His lectures abound in similes and metaphors that are redolent of the soil in which he was nurtured. Through them all runs his love for the elemental life. "I do not know of a single noise in nature that is irritating," he told one class recently.

The same quality is often shown to his friends. Once Webb and Bert Barksdale were driving across the South Plains of Texas and ascended the Cap Rock, which separates this area from the Panhandle's North Plains. It was almost twilight. Webb stopped his Plymouth and said, "Let's get out and look around and breathe LIFE."

They got out.

"Isn't it great! Can't you feel it? Can't you smell it?"

Barksdale replied that all he could feel was perspiration and all he could smell was the remnant of crop dusting.

"You're just a woodsland ignoramus," Webb snorted and returned to the car.

With a few exceptions, the best students Webb has attracted have been someone else's, so that he does not have an impressive list of his own graduates. But all over the University, in both the humanities and social sciences, the professors, many of whom have scant sympathy for history as a discipline, send their students for at least a taste of Webb. And they go out influenced by a man who has taught them that while the conclusion may be transitory the power to think for one's self can produce results that are long-lasting and satisfying.

Why did Webb become a historian? Why does he see history as an art more instinct with poetry and feeling than with traditional concepts of compilation and synthesis?

To try to answer those questions would be presumptuous. Since Webb himself probably doesn't know, the best an outsider can do is to relate how he started, and then let Webb finish the account.

At sixteen Webb had decided to be a writer, if for no other reason than to escape the hard life of the frontier which was to provide his intellectual destiny. (He once remarked that the only other routes for escape from the farm were to become a schoolteacher or a mail clerk on the Texas and Pacific Railroad.)

He planned to write fiction, but he lacked confidence. Sensitive and introspective to a fault, he experienced difficulty with English courses at the University of Texas, which discouraged him still further so that he went nearly a decade without writing anything.

By the 1920's he had received a commission to write some Texas Ranger recollections for a petroleum trade magazine, and this restored his confidence and renewed his ambition.

He then wrote — and sold — three short stories. But still he lacked confidence, and clung to teaching as a vocational buoy. Also, he says, somewhat ruefully, "I thought you had to have a fresh plot for each story."

So history, or non-fiction, the second choice, became Webb's field, because there was a solidity, a security in it. Whether he would have succeeded in fiction is anyone's conjecture, but the urge to write *something* did make a historian out of him.

He endorses three criteria for a writer — a belief that he has something to say, that it is worth saying, and that he can say it better than anyone else.

"If he ever stops to doubt," Webb says, the author "immediately loses that confidence and self-deception . . . so essential to authorship. . . .

"But back of the illusion . . . there is an insatiable, wholly unreasonable desire to write, a desire so strong that it becomes almost a pain. It is this overwhelming desire that urges the individual along the hard road of apprenticeship, that seizes on his subconscious and stores it with the method, the means, the vocabulary and above all some idea to write about. At work or at play, the author is storing up images, sorting experiences, absorbing figures of speech from what he hears, reads or observes. He is not doing this as a chore or assignment . . . he does it unconsciously, subconsciously, because he can't help it . . . because he loves the turn of a phase and the skillful projection out of the mind of an idea with clean and clear definition. Of all this stuff he makes deep in his mind . . . deeper than memory or reason . . . a compost bed, a rich soil, a matrix, out of which may come at the proper time a felicity of expression and an idea clothed with the force of truth."

None of this explains, of course, what caused Webb to devote himself to enlarging the germinal idea propounded by

Frederick Jackson Turner in 1893. The fact is that he did, and produced four books that line up in a row — the local *Texas Rangers*, the regional *Great Plains*, the intersectional *Divided We Stand*, and the international *Great Frontier*. All four of the books caused men to think — to applaud, sometimes to oppose, but always to think.

"He may or may not be a 'giant' historian," says Professor Hogan, "but he is certainly one of the very few with ideas. After all, reputations have been built on less than one idea." Or as Vice-President Ransom sees him:

Webb, despite all his academic success, his degrees and offices, has a completely *unacademic* mind. He is what I would call, without reference to Victorian morals, a *pure-thinker*. I know he has read a lot, but his reading has been often a starting process, not the kind of flower-picking the aesthetes use or the kind of woolgathering many academicians think is research. Most of us who write with a view to the past, work by making salads, compotes, mosaics, or other sorts of mixtures of what has been thought and said. Webb starts by scratching his own mind. He often arrives, it is true, at classic (and sometimes, I dare say, at trite) conclusions: but they are his.

Webb and Bert Barksdale once stopped at Tom Lea's El Paso home. Webb was about to submit his article on the West as a perpetual desert mirage — the one that got him damned by just about every Chamber of Commerce and newspaper west of the 95th meridian. Until three o'clock in the morning Lea and Barksdale argued that Webb's observations on the West were unacceptable and would lose him every last friend.

Finally Webb grunted, "I can't help it. That's the way I see it. I have to write it as I see it. And nothing is going to keep me from writing it that way."

"Did you ever have a moment when you would give anything to take back what you just did?" Webb was talking to Frank Glenn, the Kansas City bookman.

"I was visiting Houghton Mifflin in Boston," Webb continued, "and was given a copy of Walter Millis's *The Road to War* to look over. It had a beautiful jacket, all done up in vivid red. I took it across the street to the park and was sitting there on a bench with it beside me.

"A beautiful little Italian girl was playing nearby, and I watched her. She was about nine and she had a little brother about five. They were obviously poor and dirty. The little boy came over to the bench where I was sitting and his eyes fell on the book. It attracted him and he gradually moved closer to it. I reached out and drew it away.

"As I did, the little girl said just as calmly to her brother, 'Don't touch the book, it's too nice for you.'

"Not a word of resentment, just a statement of fact. If she had been mean or complaining, I wouldn't have minded, but she wasn't.

" 'It's too nice for you.'

"I would give anything to be able to live that over, and not to move the book away. It has bothered me for years."

The truth is that Webb, for all his overlay of gruffness, has an innate courtesy and a genuine sympathy that, in Harry Ransom's words, "is rooted in a good heart." It is not Old South, is completely devoid of any magnolia and wisteria qualities; neither is it Old West, for there is none of The Virginian's shy attention to other people's feelings. Ransom, no chauvinist, calls it "Old Texas."

"I have seen him, within a few hours, handle the big shot of a national foundation," he goes on, "academic people, a local businessman, a personal associate in business, and a hired hand — all with the same essential respect for their human dignity and with no thought of their jobs, titles, or incomes."

Earlier, it was pointed out that Webb failed to attract a worshiping feminine contingent the way Frank Dobie does. And yet, because women have an instinctive feeling for goodness in a man, there is a scattered following of them, invariably strong-minded, intelligent, and independent, who swear by Webb and whose minds will be influenced by him to the ends of their days.

When President Logan Wilson of the University of Texas learned of this sketch of Walter Prescott Webb, he wrote a letter expressing his interest. Because it comes as close as any estimate to capturing Webb, it is here quoted almost in its entirety.

You are right in not trying to "gild the lily." If there is to be any floral imagery, it should be something indigenous to the Southwest — perhaps a giant (and thorny) flowering cactus, rising impressively above the plains.

I share the high esteem for Dr. Webb as a man and as a scholar. And I find it difficult, as I suspect you will, to reduce his unique flavor and color to words. Outwardly an old-shoe type, he is actually a very complex person, and explaining him is even more of a task than describing him. He is a rare combination of earthiness and universality. A son of Texas if there ever was one, in appearance and general demeanor he would fit easily into a corner drugstore group in one of our small towns; yet he is a world-renowned scholar and one of the most creative minds to emerge from the 190,000 or more students who have attended the University of Texas during the past three-quarters of a century.

Walter P. Webb is the kind of man his associates enjoy as well as admire. In Austin's Town and Gown Club, for example, his comments are invariably among the saltiest, wittiest, and most telling. Even so, he always makes good sense, and I have never heard him speak just for effect or merely to turn a clever phrase.

Ungilded lily, cactus bloom, or whatever, Professor Webb is the kind of teacher and scholar we need more of. . . .

An Honest Preface
and Other Essays

by Walter Prescott Webb

An Honest Preface

E VER SINCE I started writing books I have had a desire to write a Preface which does what a Preface is supposed to do. In a Preface the author is supposed to take the reader into his confidence, let him in on a deep and mysterious secret, and tell him the truth. What the author really does is to introduce himself with an air of assumed modesty, try to forestall and fend off the critics, and persuade the reader to go on with the job and buy the book. On second thought, he pays in depreciated currency his obligations to those who did the research and typing, and in better coin his superiors on whom he hopes still to make an impression, and at the very end he nearly always says something trite about his family and their heroic fortitude during the birth of the masterpiece. There is no other public solo performance, whether in oratory, discourse, or music, with the possible exception of the comedian's, where the master of ceremony's laudatory task is usurped and bypassed so cavalierly. The author of a

Reprinted from *Southwest Review*, Autumn, 1951. Copyright 1951 by the Southern Methodist Press. All rights reserved.

Preface is, fortunately, wholly oblivious of the ridiculous position in which he habitually places himself; and more fortunately for him, his audience is equally oblivious of the humor of his situation. They both take him too seriously. And while there is no hope that the appearance of this Honest Preface will change a practice so long established, it may have the merit of being something unique in Preface literature.

The reader will understand (I am now going on with the Preface) that it had become necessary for me to write a book because the University Administration has made it plain that no further promotion or increase in salary would come without it. (The professional writer's reason would be slightly different, and would read: Because the grocer needs some more money. In last analysis the reasons are almost identical, as are Prefaces. Hereafter we will assume that this Preface is in the scholarly class.) In order to illustrate how important books are to their authors, I will cite you the case of Professor X, my colleague, who has received two promotions, one offer, and three invitations to lecture because he neglects his duties as a teacher and turns out books and articles in a hurry, but they are, in contrast to the present work, very superficial in my opinion. I also hear that he had to subsidize them and gets no royalty. On the other hand, there is Professor Y, who writes for popular consumption and gets paid at high rates for the stuff even though he is on the University pay roll full time. They say his royalty amounts to more than his salary.

This book deals with a special subject in a special way. It is very necessary for the reader to understand the point of view from which the subject is approached, and it is to be hoped that the critics will judge it in the light of what is attempted rather than what ought to have been done. The central idea of the book deals with an entirely new theory as to the relationship existing between the physical law governing the refraction of light and the incidence of the high cost of living on tenant farmers among the Esquimaux. Nobody has ever investigated this subject before, and it is my guess that the field has now been practically exhausted. My research book took me to see Einstein and the price stabilizer in Washington, both of whom told me all they knew on the subject. Einstein was particularly emphatic in his emphasis on the relativity of my conclusions, but the price stabilizer seemed more concerned about holding cowboy salaries down on dude ranches in Texas. Actually, neither one of them knows too much about my subject.

After the manuscript was written, I sent it to less well known, but competent, experts in each of the related fields. Both of them were rather severe in their criticism of my use of facts, and also of my original theory, which I doubt they understand, and therefore I ignored for the most part what they had to say. Having done this, I became concerned with the style in which the treatise is written, and submitted the manuscript to two of my acquaintances who have the reputation of being masters of the English language as it should be written for wide public consumption. One would think that such men could be of great service to the scholar, but as a matter of fact they returned my manuscript with a few perfunctory remarks which come under that nauseous head of faint praise. They may have been influenced somewhat by my telling them, in a covering letter, that while I would appreciate their help I wanted them to understand that there were two things they were not to tamper with, one being the thought and the other the language. These popular writers do not seem to grasp the inner meaning of deep scholarship.

The manuscript was also examined by the head of my department and was discussed with the dean of the college. Neither of them has the slightest notion about the importance of what I have done, but they cannot afford to admit it, and they will have to bear it in mind when the budget comes up next year. I also wrote letters to some of the leading members of other university faculties where vacancies are likely to occur in my field. While I have no intention of leaving this place, I could use an offer to advantage in getting a raise and promotion of rank. It never does any harm to advertise in this manner, and the practice is widely followed.

The following people were of some slight assistance to me in carrying out a most difficult task. Miss M clipped newspapers, Mr. N examined the government reports and made extracts, Miss O made up the list of references, Mr. P, a promising young mathematician, made the mathematical calculations and prepared the tables, Miss Q did the typing and most of the proofreading. A grant from the Esquimaux Research Fund paid the bill and gave me the necessary leisure to travel and think, and if the fund had been bigger the book would have been larger.

Finally, a word should be said about the contribution of my wife. In our early acquaintance she would listen with rapt attention to my ideas in the field of scholarship and to my most involved theories about the relation between things which superficially seem not to be related at all. She would bat her long lashes at me, nod her head in a most understanding manner, and her eyes would twinkle large with the light of her intellect. So I thought. Later, I will not name the date, she seemed to develop other interests, and actually appeared to be bored when I explained the laws of the refraction of light. She did show considerable interest in the incidence of the high cost of living, but it was not on the Esquimaux. On the whole she seems to have more immediate problems, and therefore had practically no part in this book. In that respect she is the most unusual person ever to be the wife of an author of a Preface.

What we both hope for more than anything else is that this book will sell a million copies in spite of this Honest Preface. That will be a book! The characters in this Preface are purely fictitious and if any author recognizes himself he is requested to remain quiet. As for Prefaces they usually wink at each other in passing, but they never make a fuss.

Foreword from *Texas County Histories*

Although the title would indicate that the following article is too local in interest for inclusion here, actually its subject matter covers a much wider range. Webb has a penchant for taking a purely local topic and giving it a treatment that often carries universal application. Thus, in this Foreword, Webb uses the narrow subject of Texas County Histories to analyze some of his ideas of what it means to educate.

J.B.F.

❧❧

I HAVE NEVER BELIEVED IN the foreword because it always seemed to detract from the dignity of the author and the intrinsic value of his book. If his book is good, it needs no introduction; if it is bad, no introduction can add to its merit, no flattering foreword can lift it up. But my objection does not apply to this book. This is not really a book. It is a key to

By H. Bailey Carroll (1943).

books, a bibliography. Its making does not involve the ability of the writer as a writer, his competence in style, or his profundity of ideas. There is no opportunity to talk about these qualities here.

The first thing I wish to do is to speak of the quality of the bibliographer. Certainly there can be nothing inspiring in making a list of books. It is not akin to writing a poem or a novel. It offers less outlet for the creative instinct than either biography or documented history. From any point of view it is painful drudgery and unmitigated toil. There can be no thrill of joy in the doing and there can be no material reward. I do not understand bibliographers, but I do appreciate them because of the service they render and the hard work they save me and other people. It is of this service that I can speak.

Bibliographers themselves realize, after it is too late, the troubles they have involved themselves in. Yet they seem powerless to escape from the net of their own obsession. Thomas W. Streeter speaks of this in an article which he read before the Bibliographical Society of America: "Many years ago I embarked quite light-heartedly, almost casually, on the project of compiling a critical bibliography of books, broadsides, and maps relating to Texas, 1795-1845. . . .   Raines in his *Bibliography of Texas* has taken three and a half centuries (1536-1896) for his field. I proposed to limit myself to an interesting half-century . . . it appeared to be a comparatively simple task. . . .   What then did this task for a winter's evening turn out to be? For the period, Raines cites around 200 titles. For the same period, I have assembled, and am now 'agonizing' with, upwards of 1400. I cite these personal experiences as a warning to the unwary who may feel that destiny has called on them to write the bibliography of some interesting period of a state or region. . . ."

Despite what I have said, the bibliographer often achieves

an immortality that is denied to all but a few of his contemporaries. Time does not dim the luster of a good bibliography, but improves it. After the popular novel is forgotten and the "authentic" history is out of date, the bibliography comes into its own. It finds its place on the rare bookshelf, is worn out by use in used libraries, and the perfect copy is exhibited with sadistic joy by the collector who has it to the one who wants it.

The bibliography is a scarce book by the time it is printed because the demand is so limited and the edition is correspondingly small. It soon becomes rare because it is useful. It never gets out of date for the period it covers and with time it becomes more valuable for that period. C. W. Raines' general bibliography of Texas was published, in 1896, at his own expense. This book is today one of the most prized, and most useful books in any library concerned with Texas, and is indispensable to any collector of Texana. It is quite probable that a good copy of Raines — and it needs no further description — would bring more money than he realized in profit for all his labor. The law of compensation eventually gives the bibliographer his reward, post mortem though it may be.

Dr. Carroll has indeed opened a new field in Texas bibliography by listing in one volume the titles of books and articles available on each of the 254 Texas counties. There is little doubt that this key to county histories will make a broader appeal than have most bibliographies. The reasons are not far to seek. The first one is that the book performs a service to 254 local divisions of the state, and no less for the state as a whole. A second reason is found in the convenience of the arrangement: the counties are listed alphabetically and the titles are listed under the counties. It is one thing to have a bibliography on Texas, and quite another to have a bibliography on Bexar, Deaf Smith, or Zavala County. Every editor, teacher, lawyer, and minister will find here a key to the historical literature of his own community.

It is only when we come to consider the influence that this book may have on the future that we realize the magnitude of the service here performed. Every intelligent person is, whether he knows it or not, interested in the history of his own family and community or county. When this interest becomes manifest, the first inquiries are: What material is available? Have any books been written? Who wrote them? Who published them? When and where were they published? These inquiries are made at the library, if there be one, at the newspaper office, at the school and of people who buy and read books. The information obtained is in most cases meager. The books themselves are likely to be found only in the few large libraries in the state. The result is that the curiosity of the inquirer about his own community has been baffled and he turns to something else. The presence of one copy of Dr. Carroll's book in the community would answer all the questions raised, or enough of them to encourage further effort.

If there is only one copy, it should be in the best library in the community. When the librarian learns that there is a growing demand for books about the county, she will begin to seek out the books and to buy them. They are made available to all and sundry, and especially to students in the high school. The students can now write their themes on county history because they have something to work on. They extend their investigations to the newspaper files, the court records, and by interviews to older citizens who carry valuable memories in their heads. Some of these young people become writers, and through their work knowledge of the community is further extended. In time comes the novelist to put the story in fiction. The poet puts it in verse and the painter finds that the sunset and the landscape are worthy of his art. The result is that the life of the whole community is affected. The people come to know their own lore. They prize the oak under which the first court was held or from which the horse-thief was hanged. They take pride in their own beginnings and see life around them with its third dimension. In the mean-time the books accumulate in the community, knowledge spreads about the community, and the people come to feel that they have a culture and a civilization of their own and not something borrowed or brought in from a summer trip. They will love a place, and loving it, they will take pains to improve it. Their houses will be better and their gardens more beautiful. Native things will come to be appreciated. The tree on the hill will cease to be considered as only so much firewood and the wild flowers in the pasture as more than so many weeds. The birds, solitary wasps and ants are fascinat-ing subjects for study in every community. It would be some-thing if each community in Texas could be such that the youth who leave it will carry the image of it with them and return to it however far they may wander.

Someday educators are going to learn something about edu-cation. I have said that this bibliography is only a key to books about Texas. In their turn the books are themselves only keys which admit us into the various rooms of the man-sion of real living. They are not unlike a microscope, through which we are enabled to see things too small to be seen un-aided, or the telescope, which opens up vistas of distance otherwise beyond our ken. The thing that we are after is not in the microscope or telescope, but at the end of it, in the focus. It would seem very silly to gather great quantities of microscopes and telescopes, place them on shelves and in catalogues and teach people that education could be obtained only by a study of these instruments.

Each book has a focus on some aspect of life, and its purpose is to enable us to see, not the book, but the life at which the book aims our minds and imaginations. We shall never be truly educated until we are able to see things themselves, either through the book or without it. Let me illustrate. One may know by rote a book about birds, but he can never know much about birds until he is able to go into the field, identify them, and study for himself their habits and instincts. The author of the best book might make a mistake about birds, but the birds themselves make no mistakes where their own actions are concerned. They are the only primary source on birds.

Somehow the notion has got abroad that education is confined to reservations as were the Indians. Books are gathered there and professors aggregate to read or to recommend them. The biggest reservations are called universities and it is too generally assumed that they have a sort of monopoly on knowledge and the facilities for acquiring it. What they really have is a vast number of descriptions which are called books and a somewhat lesser number of describers called teachers. We can never have real education, or a self-perpetuating culture, until we get beyond the description and the describer to the things described. In short, education needs to be got off the reservations, not only for the sake of those who go there for a four-year sojourn among the facilities, but for the sake of those who remain in closer contact with the realities.

If books are only descriptions, the only qualification needed to master them is the ability to read; and the requirement for taking in lectures is even less. It is only by looking through the microscope or telescope that we may see things worth while. It is the same with books and professors. We have assembled the mechanism of education in the universities, but fortunately we have not assembled life itself with which true education is solely concerned.

From my point of view, which always seems to me to be a most reasonable one, there is a great hidden university within a radius of five miles of every community. The geology is deeper than any well and the astronomy is firmament high. In between lie all the other branches of knowledge from the mysteries or religious experience to the mathematics of land surveys. The substance of science, art, and literature lie about and around us, things too big to be confined on the reservation. We shall have a real culture in Texas when we begin to see that this is so. Then we shall gain the right conception of the function of the university as a place to go to borrow for a time the use of the mechanisms, the descriptions, and all of the facilities with which to extend our vision and enable us to view real things with more understanding and intelligence.

Many years ago it was customary for students who were finishing college to gather around a bonfire and burn their books as a token that they were through with the tasks of learning. The custom of burning books might be revived, but with an entirely different implication. It should signify that the individual has discarded the book as he would a crutch which he no longer needed, and that he is now going forth on his own intellectual legs to examine the things which the books called to his attention but revealed so inadequately. Such a ceremony would indicate that the individual had passed from an imitative to the creative stage of existence. Education would then get off the reservation and disperse itself in a thousand centers over the land.

This bibliography is not going to effect any such revolution as I have hinted at. It is not suggested that there will be any quick transformation of the cultural pattern. Certainly no Texan, I least of all, would want Texas suddenly converted into Utopia, and thus isolated from the rest of the world. Perfection is entirely too uniform to suit a land which approaches perfection closest in its lack of uniformity. I would not flood the deserts or dry up the swamps; I would not cover the Panhandle with pine trees or remove them from the Sabine. I would not change Texas much if I could. She suits me just as she is, this eternal triangle of forest, desert, and plain. What I would do is to encourage study which would result in a better understanding and a deeper appreciation of Texas. The merit of this bibliography is that it will contribute to this end.

A word should be said about the authors who have written the 814 books and articles listed here. For the most part each has done a labor of love, and in that sense must be akin to the bibliographer himself. The task of writing local history, especially in new communities where usually only scanty records are kept, is prodigious. It requires patience in seeking out material, skill in interviewing and in harmonizing remembered events with ascertainable facts. The local historian must exercise nice discrimination between what he can tell and what cannot be told. He often must close the closet door and pretend that he did not see the skeleton grinning over the family's past misdeeds.

Since each of these authors was intimately associated with the life about which he wrote, each has contributed something to taking education off the reservation. Each looked closely at local life, found there something worth doing for its own sake, and was the better for doing it. I dare say each history, done at such close range, has taken on in some measure the color, texture, and climate of the land described. There must be a suggestion of the fantastic forms and gorgeous lights and shades that forever haunt the memory of him who has seen the counties of the Big Bend and the west. And surely these books from East Texas counties have in them the hue and flavor of red clay, the perfume of the deep forest and the sound of rain on the forest's roof of trees.

There must be wind and sun from the plains, but at night wind and sun lie in quiet together and for a while this vast land is caught in a spell of motionless silence and beauty. Each of these books is like a colored stone, and each of a different color or shade. All of them fitted together form a mosaic of Texas, and since each is in some measure true to its part, the mass is true to the whole. The general historian who can synthesize them and tell the story of Texas with the same fidelity will have written the book that Texas is waiting for. His labor will be arduous, and though this bibliography will ameliorate his labor, it will at the same time increase his responsibility to do the job well. Such a history as I have suggested, built upon the broad foundation of these titles and official sources, might serve to convey some notion of the real life of Texas to those who sojourn on the educational reservations.

It seems that what started out to be a foreword for a bibliography has developed into a theory that true education stems from the earth, from what Hamlin Garland called the verities. Any ultimate effectiveness of education depends upon a recognition of the principle and upon the application of practice to the principle. Each acre of the earth is a library, a museum, and a laboratory in which the most marvelous experiments are being carried out. The process of education is simply that of enabling the student to read the books, observe the exhibits, and witness with understanding the experiments. One who can do these things is educated regardless of whether he ever saw the inside of an institution devoted to describing them. It is in this hidden university that we have the substances themselves, the true verities, whereas on the reservations we have only specimens.

This theory is too simple to agree with those unnatural ones which have been taught. It denies that the process of education is one of pouring in, as is practiced, or of drawing out, as is preached. It does not believe that "the child is the most important factor" and that everything revolves around him. It denies the validity of pouring, drawing, or revolving as an educational process. The first results in too much full-ness, the second in emptiness, and the third in dizziness. It requires no great stretch of the imagination to think of ap-propriate degrees for each of these three schools, or to visual-ize the tripartite procession that would be certified on gradua-tion as Bachelors of Emptiness, Masters of Fullness and Doctors of Dizziness.

The name of the theory I propose is the biodynamic theory of education, or a theory of life motion. It implies a current flowing through a circuit as in electricity. Every good teacher has had experience with what I am here trying to describe. It was said that Mark Hopkins could set up such a circuit by putting himself on one end of a log and a boy on the other, which simply meant that Mark Hopkins knew how to handle his apparatus so as to make contact, start a spark, and induce a current of inquiry and learning.

The theory of biodynamic agriculture furnishes the best analogy for educational purposes. The proponents of that theory hold that the farm is not an inanimate thing, but a liv-ing organism, and that its prosperity depends on setting up the proper current to keep the organism in good health. The concept of a farm as a living thing with life currents throb-bing through it is most attractive, so attractive to me that I bought one. The circuit described for biodynamic agriculture is something like this. The land produces crops, the crops are fed to the stock, the compost and manure from the stock, re-fined by earthworms, are returned to soil. By this process a balance is maintained. If any step is neglected disaster re-sults inevitably. The farmer is the technician who keeps the wires in order and the life currents moving as they should.

Now the purpose of education — I mean real education — is to set up a current of understanding between the student and the things of the world in which he lives. In the process of learning the student begins to look at the things in the books. We say he studies, and so he does. The only purpose of his study is to get the life current of understanding started. Once it begins to flicker, he reads more books as his intellectual curiosity drives him on. It is when he is able to lay the book down and examine the rock or the star or the blade of grass for himself and with understanding that he begins to be educated. He still reads books, but only for the short cuts, to gain what advantage he can from the work of others. Once educated, he turns to things not found in universities, but at large.

He must fertilize the anemic hothouse plants of knowledge in the compost beds of nature and with the strong, acrid manures of reality before they can grow strong and bear good fruit.

In this biodynamic system of education the function of the teacher is plain. He is the farmer, the technician, whose business it is to arrange the apparatus, make the necessary contacts, and hope for the spark that sets the mysterious current going. The current flows from the student to the libraries, museums, and laboratories, and when a little stronger it takes in the greater life of which these things are but symbols. As the mind expands, the volume increases until it can no longer be confined. It goes out into the world there to be fertilized by the verities. Eventually and inevitably it returns some of its vigor to the field in which it started. Thus is the circuit complete.

This bibliography represents one step in an application of the biodynamic principle of education to history. The process seems to have started with the local histories, but each author could probably tell how the spark and the current started in him. Each felt the throb of intellectual excitement between his mind and the things, people, events he was writing about. It will be noted, too, that many of these histories started from low on the ground, from the people of whom they were written. They are very earthy, and in their earthiness they reflect truth.

The next step came when the bibliographer saw the significance of these local accounts and brought them all together in a most useful compendium of reference information. His work has its peculiar value, a unique value, because it rests on a base as broad as the dimensions of Texas and has a substantial point of contact with 254 counties.

Now we must await the historian for whom the way has been prepared to write the story of Texas, a story which ought to be true, not only in fact but in spirit and in flavor. This bibliography will never be far from his reach if he is to do what is expected. Such a book, when it comes, will complete the circuit and contribute in a thousand communities to a richer culture risen from the fertile soil of humble local histories.

The Queen's College
Oxford
November 11, 1942

How the Republican Party
Lost Its Future

Published in a literary magazine whose appeal is primarily regional, the following article received national attention. Time, for instance, excerpted large portions of it. After the 1952 elections Webb received innumerable acid comments and friendly twittings about his abilities as a political seer. With the Democratic successes at the congressional level since, Webb's critics have been quieter.

J.B.F.

❧❧

SENATOR HENRY CABOT LODGE, JR., published in the *Saturday Evening Post* of January 29, 1949, an article entitled "Does the Republican Party Have a Future?" Though he spoke with objectivity, the fact that he could ask the question indicates that he realizes the dilemma of the party of which he is a distinguished member. It is probably the first time in the history

Reprinted from *Southwest Review*, Autumn, 1949. Copyright 1949 by the Southern Methodist Press. All rights reserved.

of the party that the question has been asked in such serious-
ness. Senator Lodge believes the party has a future, but he
suggests that it can be realized only on condition that the
Republicans clean house, discard old concepts, and adopt a
program more in conformity with the will and the aspirations
of the American people. In short he implies that the house
is in disorder, that the party's present concepts are archaic, and
that its program does not mesh with popular spirit and desires.

Many thoughtful persons have tried to explain the recent
surprising defeat of the Republican party, but most of them
have been content to do so by analyzing the current situation
in terms of such factors as the labor vote, the farm vote, or
the Roosevelt vote. At least I have read no account that
viewed the present state of the Republican party down the
long gun-barrel of history. I believe that history throws a
strong clear light on the problem and makes the eclipse of a
once very powerful institution understandable.

It must be remembered that the Republican party set out
as a great crusader bent on emancipating those Americans
who were not yet free to enjoy the benefits of democratic life.
The cause was one that made a tremendous appeal to the
idealist and to the common man. The cause gathered that
strength known as moral force. The party that espoused
the cause became the champion of suffering humanity, of
freedom, of real democracy extended to all men, even the
most humble slave. There was something here of unselfish-
ness, of humanitarianism, of philanthropy, and the appeal of
it reached in some measure every man whose pecuniary interests did not outweigh his idealism. The party first appeared
in 1854 and by 1860 it had enough strength to capture the
national government.

As a result of its first success in the election of Lincoln, the
southern states withdrew from the Union, giving the Repub-

lican party its second and its greatest opportunity, that of saving the Union. In saving the Union the party proved itself able to win the hardest war the nation has yet fought, and to add to the moral prestige it had exhibited in the election of Lincoln the prestige of physical force sufficient to hold the nation together in the gravest crisis. Here was the deed that stirred the patriotism and fervor of people everywhere, cementing their allegiance to the party with something approaching blind devotion. If you believed in freedom of men, you were a Republican, or should be; and if you believed in the Union and in loyalty to the flag, you could be nothing else. Thus it happened that the Republican party emerged from the four years of civil war triumphant in the shining armor of high moral purpose and armed with the keen sword of patriotic devotion. No political party ever set out on the path of peace — to last for more than three decades — under more favorable auspices. It had found in the shortest time the political holy grail.

But there was a structural weakness in the young party, a weakness which had considerable effect on policy for ten years after the war, and indirectly for a much longer period. The party was not geographically in the beginning a national party, and this despite the fact that it had kept the nation from dividing, had saved the Union. It originated as a sectional party, drew its total initial strength from the North, gained its first national election from Northern votes, and had relatively little following elsewhere. Had its leaders inherited Lincoln's wisdom as they did his power, the party might in time have become truly national, but it never did. It has in essence always been sectional.

Because the South became so Democratic as to be known as the Solid South, it has been assumed in some quarters that the Democratic party was sectional. On the contrary it was a national party before the Civil War, through reconstruction, and remains so today. Its members were distributed over the whole nation, though for long they formed a minority in the more populous region. It was the sectional nature of the Republican party that led directly to the harsh reconstruction measures. The Republican leaders in Congress knew that they had no members in the South to speak of, and that if the southern states were permitted to return members to Congress, the Democrats would have a majority in the House of Representatives. The only safe thing they could do was to keep the Southern Democrats out until the victorious Republicans could be assured of a majority in both houses of Congress. This political party maneuver, or gerrymander, was carried out under the guise of reconstruction with the result that no Southern state really was represented in the national Congress for nearly a decade after the war closed.

In this decade the Western states were not represented either. They were not represented because twelve of them had not yet been admitted to the Union. They existed as territories, and these territories were governed and administered by the national government, in this case the Republican party. When time came for the admission of new states, every step was taken to guarantee that they came into the Republican fold. By eliminating the South and conditioning the West, the Republicans built up their strength to a point where they could safely permit the Southern states to send Democrats back to the Congress. But for a period of ten years the Republican party, operating from the Northern states, held undisputed political control in theory and in fact over the entire nation — over the South because it was being reconstructed, over the West because it was largely unoccupied and still territorial in status.

The Republican party, having gained a breathing spell by

disfranchising Southern Democrats, set itself to the task of consolidating its strength and binding its membership to it before memory of its original high idealism and its patriotic achievement in saving the Union had faded into the background. It is perhaps a good political maxim that a party cannot live by its past alone. It must make good every day, at least every administration. This the party succeeded in doing.

Its position after Appomattox is probably unique in political history: unique in that within five years from the time it came to power it had completed its program. It would be a mistake to assert that the Republican party of 1860 or 1864 had but one plank in its platform, but it is no mistake to say that it had only one that was important. The others were window dressing. By 1865 it had carried out the reform that gave it its birth and its original strength. As a reformer it had completed its mission and should have been ready to die, but the Republican party was not ready to die — as what party is? It was confronted with the necessity of finding another plank, evolving another program that would justify its existence and assure its growth. Fortunately its unlimited power and prestige at this juncture were matched by an unequaled opportunity, and that opportunity was seized with the unerring instinct which comes when the cards of success are falling right.

The whole nation lay at the feet of the Republican party for development and exploitation. The South was no longer a rival or even an obstructionist and the West was a fallow field with untouched and all but limitless resources. The nation was founded on agriculture, the farm and the plantation, but this old force was not the thing to build a program on. The South had tried that. The new force — with all its dynamic future before it — was the one for the new party to champion. The new force consisted of wheels, pulleys, belts, blades, gears, driven by water, steam, and electricity in the fabrication and distribution of goods and commodities. The North had made a considerable start in the development of technology before the Civil War, and in the war it had knocked out completely any competition that the South might have developed. It was in supreme command of the dynamic power generated by the Industrial Revolution.

The Republican party, in complete political control of the North, the South, and the West, was free to choose what it would go in for. It chose well. It embraced the new and most dynamic force, not the old agriculture which was mature and comparatively static, but rather that combination known as business, meaning manufacturing, transportation, and distribution. Here was an alliance of a sectional economic power with a coterminous political power, a partnership for great achievement.

The program followed by the Republican party was designed, whether wittingly or not, to foster with loving care the economic power and smooth the way for its eager and powerful partner to seize the material resources of the nation and concentrate control in the North, and thus to make both economics and politics sectional. The policy of the Republican party was to make the North prosperous, and as long as the North prospered, the North would give its allegiance to the party and keep it in control. "The party of prosperity" was a good slogan to soothe a whole nation, but those inside knew that the real policy was Republican prosperity.

The assets of the party after the Civil War were staggering in their immensity, so enormous that they could not help but bring relative prosperity to all sections. The business interests had in hand the technology and skill to manufacture unlimited quantities of goods, enough for the entire nation. What business needed was protection from competition, domestic and foreign, and a system of transportation that would assure distribution. Government, in control of the Republican party, could protect against domestic competition by granting patents and against foreign competition by levying tariffs. Patents cannot be considered a party measure, but as luck would have it, they turned the chief benefits to the North where patentable articles were being devised and used. The Republican party made the protective tariff a broad plank in all its platforms, and throughout the Republican era the curve of the tariff was constantly upward, higher and higher. This tariff funneled the wealth of the nation into the Republican section and built up a surplus in the national treasury which was also dispensed for Republican and Northern benefit.

Business needed railroads in order to transport the goods it manufactured to all parts of the nation, but the task of building them into the West was too great for business to undertake on its own hook. It did not need to. It called on government to finance the venture. The road to the Pacific — across the plains — was projected before the Civil War but was not built because the two sections could not agree on a route. The South wanted it; the North wanted it. Neither would yield, and so nothing was done. In 1862, with the South out of the Union, the Republican Congress authorized the building of the Union Pacific from the West into the Northern region. From 1862 until building ceased, the whole railroad system was designed to feed into the Northern section. And much of the building was done at government expense.

The government had in its possession after the Civil War two enormous tangible assets which the Republican party disposed of largely to its own benefit. The first asset and the larger one was the public lands comprising approximately one-half the continental area of the United States. Until 1862 the policy had been to sell the public lands to individuals,

but in that year of fateful and far-reaching Republican legisla-
tion the Homestead Act was passed and the lands were given
away. It was not difficult to convince any recipient of a
homestead ranging from 160 to 640 acres that the Republican
party was beneficent and worthy of support. Though small
areas were given to individuals, much larger ones were given
to corporations. The railroads received western lands equal to
the area of France. This lavish distribution of the greatest
relief fund in history to individuals and corporations took
nothing away from the popularity of the Republican party,
but it relieved the government of its landed estate and national
resources and prepared the way for another and less popular
form of relief.

The second asset in the hands of the government during
this era was cash in the treasury, cash accumulated from the
tariff imposed by the Republican party for the benefit of the
infant industries of business. The question was not one of
how this surplus cash could be returned to all the people,
but rather how it could be placed safely in the hands of the
chosen section and in the hands of good loyal Republicans.
The solution was easy, the answer almost obvious. Give it to
the Union soldiers of the Civil War in the form of pensions.
Thus would it reward loyalty and strengthen business — and
the Republican party. The pension rolls were set up during
the war and increased constantly until 1923, nearly sixty
years after the war ended. Here was a safety valve that would
relieve the treasury of its surplus.

In any attempt to account for the deterioration of the Republican party the declining influence of these pensions cannot be ignored. Not only did the receipt of a pension check
each month hold the member of the GAR to the Republican
party, but it likewise held all his kith and kin, especially those
on whom he might otherwise have been dependent, and

friends whom he might influence. That this pension money, gathered from the pockets of the entire nation, flowed mainly into the pockets of one small section, the records in Washington will abundantly prove. Of each $100 paid in pensions, about $85 went North and $15 was distributed to scattered Republicans in the South and West. Here was one of the most dependable blocs of votes that any party could hope to have.

It should not be difficult, then, to understand the loyalty of business to its political partner. Business had never known such opportunities, and nowhere in the world had it made more of the possibilities that lay before it. An increasing population in an expanding frontier lapped up all the commodities that could be produced and each year called for more. The resources were so great that there was something for all, enough to hide many inequalities. The Republican party rode this dynamic wave and won election after election. A part of its advantage was the fact that its position was positive; it was doing things, and much was being done in its name. The opposition had to content itself with blocking, interfering, and protesting. What could you do with a party that had emancipated the slave, saved the Union, given everybody a bounty in land or tariff, assured businessmen of prosperity and poor men of a full dinner pail?

The answer, as the opposition found out, was nothing — nothing but wait. The waiting was long. The South, sitting disconsolately outside the warmth of the charmed circle, sans tariff, sans pensions, was always in protest, but could be ignored. In the seventies and eighties the farmers of the West — though Republican by inheritance — raised their voices, against monopolies more than against the party that had fostered them. The Populists got nowhere. But the campaign of 1896 — foreshadowing that of 1932 — gave the

Republicans a great scare and caused them to adopt, under the leadership of the able Mark Hanna, tactics as effective as they were reprehensible in order to win. This should have been a warning.

Despite the party's splendid record of achievement, keen observers might have detected by the turn of the century the deterioration that had set in, a deterioration in position. No party can live on its memories or expect to live on gratitude for past favors. By 1900 people were a little tired of hearing that Lincoln, the only great President the party has produced, had freed the slaves. By then the Union was so well saved that even the bloody shirt no longer evoked patriotic emotions. These things lay far in the past. The giving away of the public domain lay largely in the past too, and some were saying that the policy had been carried too far. The pensioners were dying rapidly, and the political loyalty of the GAR was becoming less important. The one vital force left to the Republican party was business.

Between the close of the Civil War and the eclipse of the Republican party in 1932, business made spectacular progress. As everyone knows, it got very big and more powerful than any other factor in American life. We emphasize this in books and politics by the use of capitals: Big Business. It has already been pointed out that business was the principal ally of the Republican party, the only one that survived the passage of years and retained its vitality. It crystallized around the corporations which the Republicans got the Supreme Court to define as individuals in order to override the will of the states and other protestants. The party did everything that could be done to clear the track and give cannon-ball right of way to the business special. The Republican boast, so effective in many campaigns, of being the party of business was sound and true.

This alliance between business and the dominant political party made an unbeatable combination as long as they could deliver prosperity and keep the factory wheels turning and the people employed. With the passage of time, subtle changes began to take place in the relationship between the two partners and also within the domain of each partner.

In the beginning both partners were young, each with its special vigor, but of the two the political partner was dominant. It was the Republican party that had the political power to grant the land to the railroads, to give a tariff bonus to manufacturers, and to grant pensions to the GAR. In the process of doing this it transferred the government's wealth — which theoretically belongs to all the people — into the hands of the party section, party members, and party supporters, that is, into the hands of business. The result was that business grew very powerful and became dominant. In the beginning the party had political power and economic assets; in the end it had only political power, the assets having been transferred. Therefore when it needed economic assets it became a supplicant before a power it had formerly controlled and helped to make.

Time brought changes in business and these changes compelled the Republican party to make two hard choices, neither of which was politically wise. Shortly after the Civil War the original numerous small businesses began to merge into fewer bigger businesses, forming trusts and approaching monopolies in one field after another. In the struggle that ensued the Republican party had to choose its destiny; would it champion the cause of small business or would it go where the power and money were, with Big Business? It is doubtful whether, given the background, the Republican party could have made any choice but the one it did. The choice in favor of Big Business was natural, logical, and under the circumstances inevitable. For as a matter of fact, the men who were operating Big Business were by the time the prime movers of the Republican party. They were on the board of directors of the corporation and of the party.

Another division in business compelled the Republican party to make a second choice. With the rise of the great industries, there was a sharp division between the owners or managers and the employees who did the work; there was capital on the one hand and labor on the other. The Republican party could not champion the cause of both. Its whole history of opposition to greater or less degree to the demands of organized labor indicates its decision in favor of capital.

The important thing to notice in both of these decisions is that the Republican party threw its support to the minority as against the majority. There were more small businesses than big businesses, and there were far more laborers than there were managements or managers. Slowly but surely the Republican party was narrowing the base of popular support upon which any party in a free democratic country must in the long run depend.

After it ran out of homesteads, the Republican party had no place at all for the farmer. It may have given him lip service, but it never could accept the poignant plea of 1896 that the farmer too was a businessman. He was something else, a farmer. Even if it had granted him the status of a businessman, the party would have classed him as a small businessman, and his interests would still have been made secondary to those of Big Business. Throughout it compelled him to buy in a protected market and permitted him to sell in a free market with all the world as his competitor. For the farmer's mule or cow or cotton or tobacco there was neither tariff nor patent.

It is difficult to explain the long record of loyalty of Middle

Western farmers to the Republican party, why they clung to it for three-quarters of a century to the detriment of their own welfare. The most reasonable explanation is that they inherited their Republicanism. The fact that their fathers received free homesteads and pensions brought them into the party and a loyal inertia held them there for a very long time — but not for ever. They woke up at last to the fact that the party had done nothing for them lately.

Thus the Republican party successively turned its back on one great segment of society after another, on the farmer, on small business, on labor. The party quit the people long before the people quit it. Finding Big Business a jealous god, it gave it complete and undivided devotion, sacrificing its Lincolnian idealism and its early patriotic fervor for the down-trodden man, and thus cutting from under itself the foundation on which popular support could with any reason stand. It is not surprising that the Republican party eventually went down in defeat known to no other major party in history; the surprising fact, the one that needs explanation, is that its defeat was so long delayed. The explanation of the delay must be sought in the unbroken success of business.

The party was never really defeated in the sense that it lost prestige, until its main partner — and we might almost say its only one — collapsed. Since business near the end was the only ally of strength the party had, the condition for the continued dominance of the party hinged on the ability of business to provide prosperity. It was business that had to make and distribute the goods, maintain employment, and provide hope for the future. As long as business did this, the voters went along voting the Republicans into power with only an occasional interlude by protesters and reformers.

The union of business and the Republican party was never more felicitous than in the years following World War I. It is quite true that one President was not quite up to the standard expected, but the two that followed were well-nigh perfect. President Hoover, the engineer and humanitarian, was the ideal man for the party of business. And business was so good during the early part of his administration that the Republicans promised to make prosperity permanent and to put two cars in every garage. It would be hard to beat a party that does either.

Then it happened, overnight. The bottom fell out, not of the Republican party, but of business. From 1929 to 1933 the administration — representing the Republican party — moved around in a daze, completely stunned by the disaster that had come to its partner and main support. Though there was some vague talk about turning a corner, the Republicans were never able to make the turn. Their policy had been to let business take its course, and it was perhaps too much to expect a sudden reversal of a time-honored and well-established system.

In the next election the Republican party had nothing on which to base a campaign. Born on a platform of one plank, slavery, it died on a platform of one plank because that plank, business, had decomposed and fallen from under it. It began as a sectional party, carrying only northern states; it died as a sectional party carrying six states, all of them in the region of its original strength. Four years later it carried Maine and Vermont. Gone from it were the farmers of the Middle West, gone the votes of the laboring men, now jobless, around the silent factories of the industrial North. Gone also the tradition of invincibility and the belief that the Republican party alone knew the magic formula of prosperity and success.

The collapse of business in 1929 and of the Republican party in 1932 gave the opposition the first opportunity it had had since long before the Civil War to seize the initiative and

launch a constructive program. It is true that in a period
of seventy-two years, from 1860 to 1932, the Democrats won
four elections, serving sixteen years to fifty-six for the Republicans. But none of these victories gave the Democrats a
broad initiative. They were due in Cleveland's case to protests
against Republican rule, and in Wilson's case to disaffection
in the Republican party and to war. The foundation under
the Republicans in each case remained strong and sound, and
as soon as the reformers had failed in their reforms, control
slipped back into safe Republican hands. The party still stood
for the constructive force, the development of business, and
not for the complainers, obstructionists, and amorphous dis-
sident elements which have always been a plague to the out
party.

The entry of the Democratic party in 1932 was a triumphant entry such as it had not known before. Not only had
the opposition been defeated, but its old sources of strength
lay in complete ruins about it. The task was to build from the
ground up on another principle. Twice before the Democrats
had had the ball but had not known what to do with it. This
time they had the ball and, as it turned out, they knew how
to keep it, and what to do with it.

What the Democrats did after 1932 was to launch a bold
program much greater than but comparable to the one under-
taken by Lincoln. And that program was based on an entirely
new principle. The forces of government were directed, not
to the restoration of business alone, but toward the rehabilita-
tion of the suffering and destitute of the entire nation. It was
in the words of Roosevelt himself a "crusade to restore
America to its own people." That was a long-range program.
In the short range it would give bread to the hungry, clothes
to the naked, fuel to the freezing, jobs to the jobless, security
to the aged, and insurance to the bankers; and, having no
public domain to give away and no other government assets, it

would pay for all this by taking money away from those who had it, mainly from Republicans and Big Business, and giving it to those who needed it. It was the taking and not the giving that stirred the bitterness and acrimony, just as Lincoln's taking away property in slaves had stirred it three-quarters of a century earlier.

In this analysis we are not concerned with the merits of the program, its constitutionality, or its rightness or wrongness. We are concerned with its political effectiveness, with the broad appeal it had for the majority and its seemingly utter disregard for the powerful minority. This program gave the Democrats an initiative based on a new principle which for the time being the Republican party cannot possibly take from it and remain the Republican party. The Republican party for the first time in its history is now definitely on the outside. It can only complain, criticize, claim it can do the job better and more efficiently. It has as yet nothing constructive to offer, and under the present conditions it seems doubtful whether it can find anything to offer that its members would accept or the American voters would take at face value. The Republican party worked out to the last grain its vein of success and for the present it is through. It carried to a logical conclusion the policy of taking from the many — either the government or the people — and giving to the few, taking from the three sections and giving to the favored one. Here was a principle that was good as long as it lasted, but it was not an eternal principle. Senator Lodge refers to archaic concepts of the party, but I would like to suggest to him that the great principle of the party is archaic and that therefore practically everything about it is now out of date. The old place may be tidied up a bit, but it will still be a Victorian palace with its gingerbread and gewgaws showing.

By way of being specific let us examine some of the cherished details of the establishment — relics of a dead past

— that have no place save in a political antique shop. The first of these is the front porch. Now in its day that was quite an institution. It was a comfortable place for the presidential candidate who was sure of election to reside in dignity while the opposition beat its brains out trying to gain the attention of spellbound voters. It was a good place from which to make no mistakes, commit no errors. The front porch is one antique that the Republicans will have to give up until they get a house to go with it.

Another outworn formula has to do with the off-year elections. This formula held that if in the rare Democratic innings the Republicans gained control of Congress in the off-year election, that was a sure sign that the Democratic President was on his way out, come next election. In 1946 the Congress became Republican and it was taken for granted that the formula would work. The White House was as good as won.

So eager was the Eightieth Congress to please its favored constituents that it jumped the gun and began the work of destroying the principle which the Democrats had adopted and practiced for sixteen years. The result was that this Congress frightened the farmers, resolved labor's doubts, and lost the election of 1948. The formula did not work.

In the last election we did not hear much about the full dinner pail and sound money, the first a bauble for the workingman and the second a booby trap for small businessmen. For three years the workingman looked into the pail and found it always empty. And as for sound money, the Republican party ran out of money of any kind as did most of the voters. It appears that the dinner pail has been lost now and sound money, if not forgotten, is never mentioned.

It is customary for losers to quarrel among themselves in trying to apportion the blame for their defeat. According to news reports this jowering is going on now in the party high command. It seems that Mr. Dewey, who would have been so great if he had won, is taking the brunt of the attack. It may be pointed out that Mr. Dewey's whole campaign was in the very best Republican tradition. He conducted himself with the utmost propriety, said very little, and might even have remained on the front porch so far as results go. He was careful not to be specific or forthright but to depend on his supporters to make the commitments. He could not be expected to go over to the left of the Democrats, and his own party would not have followed him had he done so. His position was to the right of Mr. Truman's, and Mr. Truman's position was anchored firmly in the middle of the new principle of government. Actually Mr. Dewey had no principle. He was simply trying to get the voters to shoulder Mr. Truman out of his position, and the stubborn voters flatly refused to do it.

Nor can the Republicans find an alibi for their last defeat in the personality of the opposition. The two candiates were just about a hoss and a hoss in personality, though the man from New York is a little slicker than the man from Missouri. Certainly Mr. Truman's personality is not such as to give the opposition an inferiority complex. The people voted on the issues and not on the men.

President Truman's victory was so spectacular as to obscure important aspects of the last election. Had Mr. Truman been elected on personality, he might have found himself faced with a Republican Congress and with Republican governors in control of a majority of the states. The inarticulate but interested voters admired his courage and the desperate fight he made with practically nobody in his corner, but they did not vote for him through sympathy. They had simply had enough of the other party as it exhibited its program in the Eightieth Congress to know that they wanted no more of it. Wanting a modern government that will deal with modern problems and not an antiquity, they went to the polls and swept the little champ back to the White House, and with him they sent Democrats to Congress and into the governors' offices across the nation.

Of course we need two parties to debate the issues of the nation. It seems from our own political history that the debate swings around a principle. One party thinks the principle is right and the other is equally convinced that it is in great part wrong. The party that originates the principle and establishes it, does so in a national crisis. If the nation comes out of the crisis, the principle is accepted and the people go on supporting it for a long time, say until it runs into a crisis. This is what happened to the Republican party after the Civil War; it is what happened to the Democratic party in the Great Depression. During the time of trust and confidence in the principle, the party that originated it and put it into effect has a tremendous advantage, such an advantage that it may get away with almost anything. As long as the principle being acted upon works, it is almost impossible to dislodge the party that discovered it. This the Republicans need to bear in mind. They are going to have thin pickings until the present principle of developing a social state has failed. They are going to beat their brains out trying to get the attention of voters. They are going to quarrel, divide, complain, and criticize.

Their plight is like that of the man who had spent his life preparing for the future. It was his obsession. He awoke one morning on his birthday and began to appraise himself, his age, which was considerable, his hair, which had grown thin, his muscles a little flabby now, and his bones, which seemed to have sand grains in the joints. After some contemplation, he struck his hand to his head and exclaimed, "Heavens! This is my future!" And so it may be for a considerable period with the Republican party.

Coca-Cola and Culture

I n 1949 the University of Texas installed Coca-Cola dispensers in most of the buildings on its campus. Webb exploded.

"I want the milk concession," he told an administration official. When the official failed to perceive Webb's humor, Webb asked him, "Well then, what about Vat 69?"

The result was the following screed, typed out in anger. Webb took his manuscript to the front office with the announcement that he would find a publisher for it. The administration urged him not to publish it, that it would affect the University's public relations badly. Webb, who underneath is a great institution man, finally agreed. (Incidentally, the official who led the plea to withhold later left the University. On his way out, he asked Webb to give him a copy for a souvenir!)

Much later the student newspaper, the Daily Texan, obtained a copy and published it, but by then a new administration had taken over and the piece was little more than a bit of social commentary. Webb then sent a copy to E. D. Sledge,

Reprinted from the *Daily Texan*, September 26, 1957.

the Coca-Cola Company advertising manager, who replied on July 5, 1956: "One thing of which I feel reasonably confident, namely, that things aren't nearly so bad now as they were then. Otherwise, you would have departed history and the University of Texas a long time ago."

Mr. Sledge was correct. "Things" were better and Webb and Coca-Cola were at peace.

J.B.F.

❧❧

I DESIRE TO BE HEARD for a few moments on the subject of Coca-Cola and higher education, with the main emphasis on the drink that refreshes. My purpose is to protest the location of Coca-Cola machines in University classroom buildings, and to request that they be removed from the first floor of Garrison Hall if not from other places.

My association with Coca-Cola is one of long standing, going back to the days when it could be obtained only in drugstores at a price which never varied. I had evidence of its distracting influence years ago when driving north from Austin; there loomed in the curve of the road, beyond the state hospital, a huge signboard adorned by a creature of most beautiful proportions in the act of partaking of this wonderful drink. I almost failed to make the bend and barely escaped wrecking my car. From that time I have been wary of Coca-Cola and its influence for good in the world. Never did I suspect that it would force its way into the entrance of my building, and almost into my office on the first floor of Garrison Hall.

Early this fall men in caps, equipped with augers, gimlets, saws, and rolls of wire, began to hack and hammer at the masonry and tile in Garrison Hall, and in due time in came the big red Coca-Cola bin to be installed in front of my office door adjacent to the water fountain. This arrangement created so much congestion that the hall was impassable. People who wanted a legitimate drink could not get to the fountains. Shortly the men with gimlets and augers and hammers came back and with great clatter defaced another section of the building, and this time installed *two* machines just inside the front entrance. The traffic on the first floor of Garrison Hall is bad enough under normal conditions, especially at 10, 11, and 12 o'clock. With twenty or thirty or fifty students working the slot machines and as many more gazing at the ceiling over an upturned bottle the situation could hardly be worse.

Scarcely a day passes that a bottle does not crash on the tile floor. At intervals the attendants come to refill the machines with a noise only a little less objectionable than the rattle of small arms. They are supposed to do this in the ten-minute interval, but actually they do not, and often cannot. One teacher in G. H. 100 found it necessary to leave his class and request the attendant to cease the racket. The hall is further filled up with cases for the empty bottles, but not all bottles are placed there. Many are carried into classrooms, and some are overturned, making extra work for the already overworked force of janitors. If I wanted to make a strong argument against what is going on, I would contend that this Coca-Cola business is a piece of institutional brutality to a group of men and women who cannot complain or help themselves. They sweep and mop and gather bottles and broken glass in bitter silence.

To say that this innovation in folly does not affect the quality of teaching in this institution is to miss the truth by a mile. I know it affects my teaching, and I want to cite a case in point. Last Friday (October 14) I held a class in G. H.

111. It required about a week for me to convince the class that there was to be no smoking, but I had said nothing about drinking. About the time I started lecturing, a youth on the front row, somewhat exhausted no doubt from his exertions of the previous hour, began to refresh himself. He held the bottle in loving hands, one eye on me, the other on the bottle, as if daring someone to take it away from him. He reminded me of an eighteen-month-old boy who was very hungry. The picture he made might be appropriately entitled the atavism of a junior. Well, I did not take his bottle away from him, but I think I succeeded in taking away his appetite for it. I didn't like the job, and I don't like that part of a great institution which imposes such a job on me. The work of both teachers and janitors is sufficient without having it increased by Coca-Cola.

What reason can be given for installing these machines and creating a nuisance, if not a hazard? I can think of three reasons: (1) to promote education; (2) to promote the convenience or pleasure of the students; and (3) to make money. Now if there were a professor of Coca-Cola in the appropriate department or school of this institution I am sure he could develop a philosophy and prove to the satisfaction of his sponsor that the present arrangement does promote education, or adds to the convenience and longevity of the students, and that the service is rendered at considerable financial sacrifice on the part of a beneficent and social-minded business institution. But it is not too difficult, even for an unendowed professor, to form his own opinion as to the real motive of the Coca-Cola Company.

But what of the motive of the University of Texas? What is it trying to do? Do those responsible for the installation of these machines believe that they promote the purposes for which this university was founded? I should like to hear their arguments. Would they contend that this is all that is needed to make this a university of at least the second class?

Was it the purpose of the University to add to the convenience and pleasure of the students and faculty? If this is the aim, then the project stopped far short of the possibilities and needs. Maybe the big red boxes blocking the entrance to Garrison Hall represent the best that can be done in the old buildings, but new and expensive buildings are under construction. Why not put a great Coca-Cola vat on the roof with a system of copper tubing running to every seat and the professor's desk so that all could partake of something more agreeable than economics, calculus, and mechanical drawing? The complications arising in the fine arts department where a student undertakes to play the piano and drink Coca-Cola is a detail with which the historian is not concerned. Of course this improved system, as well as the present one, ignores the matter of individual desire. And what of the student, or faculty member, who prefers another drink, such as milk, beer, or scotch and soda? Why discriminate against him?

Finally, is it the purpose of the University in installing these machines to make money? Perish the thought! The function of the University is to give and not to receive. If the purpose is to make money out of the faculty and students, there are many and better opportunities. Other concessions should be granted on the campus, and for monopoly rights such as Coca-Cola enjoys many companies would be glad to pay a bonus. These concessions could then be auctioned off along with the oil leases.

To be sure such a system would be a little hard on free enterprise, which I am sure the Coca-Cola Company and the University believe in. Evidence that Coca-Cola believes in free enterprise is written all over its bottles and boxes. For example, it created a swivel-hipped bottle which it patented,

No. D-105,525, so that no other free enterprise is free to use
it. Then it uses a box which will hold no other bottle, which
no other free enterprise can use. The other free enterprisers
are warned that the box is patented, U.S. 229027, Canada
413,908, and, I quote, "other U.S. and foreign letters patent
pending." Thus does Coca-Cola warn twice on every bottle
and box that it believes in enterprise free from all competition.
Apparently the University believes in the same sort of enterprise, and proves it by granting an air-tight monopoly on the
forty acres to nearly twenty thousand customers. The other
cold-drink people, and the little merchants around the campus, must be delighted at such institutional impartiality.

If the University's purpose is to make money out of Coca-
Cola, I have no knowledge of what use is to be made of the
money. I dare say it is for some good cause. Now I have no
quarrel with good causes, but I do hold that a great university
has a specific function to perform, and I feel that it should
be performed with some dignity. Certainly the university
should not create conditions which interfere with the decent
processes of teaching and learning. Therefore I specifically
request that the proper authorities remove at once from the
entrance of Garrison Hall the machines which make an in-
tolerable situation, and I suggest that it may be desirable to
remove them from all University classroom buildings.

Physics, History, and Fate

As I EXAMINED the program of the annual meeting of the American Physical Society of 1954 I was struck by the exclusive concern of the members with what may be called immediacy. The papers seemed to deal primarily with problems now in the process of solution. Nowhere did I find that the physicists are concerned with perspective, past or future, with where their subject came from or whither it is going. The practicing physicists seem little concerned with the relation of their subject to the world that lies around it. I shall attempt here to place the subject of physics in its historical context, to show that it arose under peculiar historical conditions, that it grew to its present importance under conditions singularly favorable to it, that those happy conditions are now being modified, and that physics in the future may find the going much harder than it has been during its whole history as a science.

It is not strange that physics has thus far disregarded its

Reprinted from *Physics Today*, September, 1954. Copyright 1954 by the American Institute of Physics. All rights reserved.

own history, and that of civilization itself, because it has been too busy making history and shaping the civilization. The first contributions of physics were wholly favorable to mankind. As long as physics worked in constructive ways — as it did for a considerable time — the men who set its forces in motion could go about their business, tend their laboratories, and not worry about consequences so beneficial. But when the consequences begin to threaten the welfare, and even the existence of civilization, the physicists can no longer be indifferent. When, however, they seek a border view, trying to see the relationship of what they have done and will do to all that is around them, to civilization itself, they become historians, and they enter into a realm quite different in both its intent and method from the one in which they have been accustomed to operate.

In approaching physics historically, it is necessary to state the historian's function and his method. His function is to view society — dispassionately if he can — and explain its past actions with as much reason and as little passion as possible. He is, as distinguished from the physicist, severely handicapped in his method. His handicap is that he must seek truth without benefit of laboratory. Since he has no laboratory, can in the nature of his material have none, has no possible way of demonstrating by experiment, the historian can never prove anything in the sense that the physicist can. The historian does collect evidence, usually in the form of records of what happened, but he can never prove that the records are infallible or that he has all the pertinent evidence. Furthermore, he can never divest himself of his own point of view. For these reasons the historian's conclusions are always tentative, never universally accepted, and are almost certain to be discarded partially or totally by his successors. This whole procedure must seem highly unsatisfactory — and unscientific, as indeed it is — but the historian has no choice but to use it. For him there is no other method.

What the historian does as he peers into the kaleidoscopic past is this: he tries to see relationships among the varied past activities of man. He searches for connections, appraises forces and treats them as causes operating to produce resultant effects. If the historian looks at the shifting scene long enough — never directly but through other men's records — he begins to see patterns forming; a sort of crystallization seems to occur as the lens of his mind takes focus. Though these may be lovely patterns, they are more intangible than the stuff physicists deal with. The patterns can never be touched or tested by the senses; they can only be described as they appear to the informed and questing mind. Since the historian must depend on the skill of his description, the clarity of his exposition, he must give more attention to the art of presentation than his scientist brother needs to give. If he is less of a scientist, he may be more of an artist.

Once the patterns form, the historian begins to seek out the one pattern for special attention, usually the one that seems to him to dominate the age he is trying to understand. This pattern takes on importance for him; he is likely to think that he has discovered some force or influence that controlled some things, that seemed to touch and color everything in the society that it accompanies.

At this stage the historian is likely to become excited, if not slightly possessed, at the prospect. If he be daring enough, and disregardful enough of his reputation for safe mediocrity, he does what the real scientist does: he sets up a working hypothesis which holds that a certain ingredient of history, the factor that concerns him, has helped to shape mankind's action and helped direct history throughout the period of its presence. Having formulated the hypothesis, the historian hunts all available evidence to support it, re-fute it, or modify it. If the evidence does in general support the hypothesis, if nothing is found to refute it, the hypothesis is launched as a thesis in a book or an article for the critical appraisal of colleagues and the scholarly world.

It would be a great comfort to the historian if he could bolster his case with a record of controlled experimental demonstrations, all of which point to his major conclusion. This he can never do; he must always submit his case to the court on circumstantial evidence. It is not often that a sci-entist launches a thesis that he has not proved, that he has not demonstrated in the laboratory, that he has not sup-ported by figures as convincing as the multiplication table. It may be suggested, however, that there are exceptions, and notable among them are Charles Darwin and Albert Einstein.

The question arises as to how a thesis supported by cir-cumstantial evidence ever achieves validity. *How* does the high court decide whether the interpreter has made his case? *When* does the court decide? The last question as to *when* is easiest answered. There is rarely, if ever, a quick decision. The court — which is the public — ponders the case a long time, often engages in acrimonious argument and the best the historian ever gets is a split decision.

The thesis or interpretation can eventually find a measure of acceptance by meeting certain tests. The chief test is whether the explanation offered gives *meaning* to the past, whether it proves useful in enabling others to see some order in the welter of facts and conflicting opinions. If it does es-tablish a sort of intellectual life line, a control point from which the mind may take off and to which it may return, the hypothesis is likely to find wide acceptance. If things fit into the explanation, fall into place like blocks in a puzzle, and if there are not too many blocks left over, the thoughtful reader will say: "This stuff makes sense to me." If it makes enough sense to enough readers, then in time the work may be referred to as standard, a classic. This is what has happened to the theses of Adam Smith, William Graham Sumner, and Charles Darwin. We still do not know that the histories written by these men are correct, but what they wrote has been so useful, so illuminating, and so suggestive that they are still spoken of with great respect. They have achieved a practical validity, but by a process much slower and more tentative than is often the case in demonstrable science.

The method of investigation described above is one I followed in launching some months ago the thesis of the Great Frontier. The high court is now wrangling mildly over it, and only time — about twenty years — will tell as to its fate. Naturally I think the thesis has validity in that it explains some things about the modern world better than other interpretations. Naturally I would have to hold this opinion to justify the years spent in elaborating the idea and tracing out the pattern of the Great Frontier. My view of physics and other modern sciences is that which one gets when these subjects are viewed from the vantage point of the Great Frontier.

The thesis advanced is that one of the powerful forces operating on Western civilization since 1500 has been the Great Frontier. And the Great Frontier is identified as all the new lands of the Western world discovered by Columbus and his associates around 1500. It comprised North and South America, Australia, a large part of Africa, and thousands of islands scattered over the oceans. In a brief span of time the discoverers brought these continents and these islands and laid them as a free gift in the lap of impoverished and crowded Europe. As a physicist might view it, they brought a new element, a strong ingredient of gigantic proportions, a new force of immense power and strength and suddenly injected it into the society of Western civilization. These new lands — the Great Frontier comprising half of the earth — consisted of a vast body of real estate and wealth of all descriptions, lands thinly occupied by primitive peoples whose claims were lightly regarded. In effect, these continents and this wealth became the property of the nations of western Europe in a historical instant.

As a result of the injection of such an ingredient, there occurred a tremendous shift in the historical currents. Before the injection, the main forces of Western history lay *within* Europe. After the injection Europe was but one factor while another of equal potency and quite different character lay outside in the Great Frontier. These were two poles of a new, enlarged, and electric field. The drama of Western history from then until now — for four and one-half centuries — has been in the interaction between these two poles and the culture we know today is largely the product of that interaction.

Let us change the figure of speech and represent modern history as a tapestry woven in a continental frame, the continent of Europe on the right and the Great Frontier on the left. The interaction is like the shuttle going to and fro down the centuries — in migration, trade, commerce, and war — weaving fantastic patterns of man's activities over a vast area and a long period of time. In the varied patterns of that tapestry we see blended the elements of the Metropolis of Europe and elements of the Great Frontier, the warp and woof of modern western culture.

Against the background of the tapestry woven of these components, we see modern man devising institutions, ideas, and practices suitable to the new situation, such institutions as capitalism and democracy, the novel idea of progress, the

practices of rampant individualism and the marvelous unfold-
ing of a romantic literature to glorify through the imagination all that was going on. We also can see, if we look for it,
the rise of most unusual opportunities for the rapid development of pure and applied science. It is the situation existing
in this age that gave physics and chemistry their big chance
to become profitable and practical arts.

This Age of the Great Frontier, extending from 1500 to
1950, falls into two divisions. The first may be called the Age
of the Open Frontier, a long period lasting from 1500 to
about 1900. The second, the one we are now in, may be
called the period of the *closing* frontier, a mere introduction
to a longer period that lies before us, the Age of the Closed
Frontier. Since we are now only in its beginning, we cannot
with any confidence foretell what the Age of the Closed
Frontier will bring. But there is one thing of which we can
be quite sure: the Age of the Closed Frontier will be very
unlike what we have known in modern times. We are now
in revolution in the Western world, a revolution marking the
transition from the Age of the Open Frontier to that of the
Closed Frontier. In retrospect this revolution may appear as
our fumbling attempts to adjust our lives and institutions to
the imperatives of a frontierless society.

Let us turn now to consider the first and longer period
when the frontier was open. We like to say that it was dynamic, capitalistic, and democratic. Each of these features of
the modern age can be related to the Great Frontier.

A dynamic society is one that is moving, going places, and
doing things. Of such a society we say — and the term is
quite modern — that it is making progress. Physics teaches
that dynamism or a current sets up in the physical world
when for any reason there is an imbalance. Who will doubt
that the sudden injection of the Great Frontier into the

fairly stabilized society of western Europe created just such an imbalance, destroyed equilibrium, and set in motion currents of adjustment which made the society dynamic? A clear example of this imbalance may be found in the upset land–man ratio. Late medieval Europe had a fairly stabilized ratio of about twenty-six persons per square mile. Then came the Great Frontier, making available more than twenty million square miles of land occupied by very few people. The old equilibrium was destroyed, and the currents of migration began to flow from Europe to the new lands to restore the balance, and this flow, unchecked until after World War I, created a dynamic situation.

A second imbalance set a current of a different character flowing in the opposite direction. The Great Frontier was a land of vast resources much desired by those who remained in Europe. So, as the surplus people went out to the Great Frontier the wealth of that fabulous land began to flow back on Europe, and the stream mounted continuously until all Europe — and especially those portions which had access to the new lands — was inundated with prosperity. In the general ferment the philosophers advanced the idea of progress and new classes arose to overturn old governments and set up new ones more in harmony with the needs of a dynamic and thriving society.

As for capitalism, it comes easy when both men and wealth have such high mobility. Capitalism is an acquisitive game played by men who are free to act. The game was possible because the potential wealth was so abundant and because the real wealth was increasing faster than the population was growing. The game of playing for profit was interesting, exciting, and rewarding. The circumstance of vast potential wealth in one place and many poor but eager people in another justified the coming and going and made possible the return of enough successful winners to keep the tables full. There was, temporarily, sufficient potential wealth in the Great Frontier for everybody to play at getting some of it.

The rise of capitalism was further stimulated by the introduction of frontier gold and silver in quantities unknown before. The first act of the Europeans was to tap the gold and silver storehouses of the New World. From 1500 to 1650 the precious metals poured into Europe, not by the shipload, by the fleetload. Whole armadas were used by the Spaniards to transport it. This flood of gold and silver upset the ratio existing between the amount of money available and the number of people to share it, between the amount of money and the quantity of goods available. The result was a price revolution based on metals comparable to the one we have had in the last generation based on paper. In the ups and downs of that revolution, according to John Maynard Keynes, modern capitalism was born.

The over-all effect of the advent of the Great Frontier may be summed up by saying that the sudden injection of excess land, excess wealth, excess gold and silver into an acquisitive society created a general boom of gigantic proportions and long duration. The boom lasted so long that we have come to think of it as the normal state, but in reality it was — as all booms are — abnormal. The frontier kept it going for four centuries because it kept the currents of wealth pouring back on the acquisitive and eager society. In this boom men came to believe they had hit the high road to eternal progress and ever increasing prosperity. In the exceptional circumstances and excitement the laws relaxed, the old restraints fell away, and the individual as the principal actor attained an importance he had rarely known before and may not know again. Democracy was born, became the favorite form of political organization, and made its way steadily against all other forms.

The accelerating wealth was sufficient to pay for any mistakes, to permit laxity in government, and to provide broad tolerance for human frailty. All deficits were made up by cutting the Great Frontier up into shares and selling the stock on a rising market. Our present economic, political, and social institutions formed themselves in and around the boom and served well that which nourished them. There, in a paragraph, is the over-all view of this dynamic Western society during the long period when the Frontier was open, say from 1500 to 1900 or 1914.

It was in this booming period that the art of physics had its origin and its first opportunity to serve mankind in practical ways. That booming world so full of the stuff that physics works with was an ideal world, made to order with a high premium on what physics had to offer. That world was a physicist's paradise. So much for the rise.

During this abnormal period of expansion and boom two assumptions, both false, came to be accepted as truth. The first was that there would always be a frontier, that it was permanent and not temporal. The corollary to this was that the sources of wealth were also unlimited, and that all we need be concerned with was the method and means, provided largely by applied physics, of acquisition and use. Supply, it was assumed, would automatically equal demand. The second assumption was that the boom was normal, so normal that most men did not realize its existence.

Turning to the period of the closing frontier, the last half century, we find ourselves standing face to face with our previous assumptions, beginning to see how utterly false they are. There will not always be a frontier, and there cannot be an everlasting boom derived from a source that is disappearing. True, there is still an imbalance of population between the Metropolis of Europe and the Great Frontier countries, but immigration laws have cut off the current of adjustment. There is still an imbalance of wealth, the Frontier countries having most of the raw materials; the currents of adjustment are still flowing from here to there, but so sluggishly that we have resorted to the force pump. The natural dynamics that operated effectively during the centuries of the Open Frontier have either been stopped artificially or made to flow artificially. Under these changed conditions, our boom-born institutions have run into crisis after crisis. Both democracy and capitalism have been in trouble since the first world war, and both have given ground for the first time in the modern era. There is now little excess room for the explosive increase in population and there is not enough food in the world for what we have. Who will say that the present situation would not be relieved if some Columbus would enter here and announce that he had brought us three or four rich and empty continents? Then we could be sure of a new lease on the life of the frontier boom, a new lease on the same kind of life we have been accustomed to lead. As it is we find ourselves dressed up in frontier clothes, fully equipped with a fine set of frontier ideas and institutions, and nowhere to go. We are now arrived near the end of an adventurous and exciting age, and our main problem is one of making adjustments to another age that is quite different in character.

Thus far I have said little about physics, though I have tried to picture the conditions surrounding its origin and accompanying its development. I have said that his booming world, full of movement and loaded with materials, was a physicist's paradise, but I also suggested that this paradise was abnormal, a pleasant purgatorial anteroom to a less abundant future state. It is not unthinkable that physics, like democracy and capitalism, may be given pause by the closing of the frontier and the end of the boom, that it too may bog down.

In the midst of the boom, physics found unlimited opportunity to become practical, to apply its abstract principles to daily tasks. In its early stages it was concerned primarily with two elements, which I will make bold to call substance and energy. Its practical task was to apply the energy to the substance in such a manner as to procure or produce what would be useful to men. It performed this task so well that it set off a current in history that accelerated the revolution in history that accelerated the revolution in human living more than anything else known. I refer to the industrial revolution, the first stages of which belonged almost exclusively to applied physics.

What I wish to call attention to is the close connection that existed between applied physics and the Great Frontier. I have said that applied physics deals with energy and substance. The energy used in the modern age has been mainly from the fossil fuels. The Great Frontier is rich in the fossil fuels, having about 54 per cent of the world's coal and 54 per cent of petroleum. Europe has coal, but is almost destitute of petroleum. As for substance, stuff to be fabricated and moved, the United States probably has more than western Europe. In short, the Great Frontier has supplied more than half the energy and a far greater proportion of the substance with which applied physics has worked its magic.

It was in the frontier, in the United States, that physics found the most favorable conditions for a practical demonstration of what it could do. Here men were few, laborers scarce, wages high, and resources abundant. Consequently there was a premium on any device that would convert the resources into wealth with a minimum of human labor. Energy and substance being abundant and demand being great during this period, men could incur any expense that would create machines and provide the power to drive them. As a result the United States in the nineteenth century became an enormous laboratory of applied physics, and a further result of that was an accumulation of wealth equaled only by the destruction of resources.

During this happy period physics — or physicists — shared the false assumptions that both energy and substance were unlimited, that there was plenty more on the frontier, and that there would always be a frontier. Under present conditions physics faces the task of performing its services in a world of disappearing fossil energy and of declining substance.

Let us look at energy as represented by the fossil fuels. We may not know how much of it there is, but we do know that the total in storage is an absolute amount and that it cannot be increased by any art yet known to man. We also know that our use of fossil fuels is comparatively recent, and that its destruction is proceeding at an ever accelerating rate. Its total destruction, under the present process, is not only inevitable but in sight. Waldemar Kaempffert in the *New York Times* of September 20, 1953, wrote:

> Palmer Putnam of the Atomic Energy Commission turned up at Madison, Wisconsin, last week to tell the American Institute of Biological Sciences the now familiar story of the day when there is no more coal, no more oil and no more gas. What shall we do then for energy? . . . Putnam saw no salvation in atomic energy . . . We have about three centuries to engage in research and experimenting . . . time enough to devise something that will work. There is no doubt that when the world stands face to face with no combustible fuel and no uranium or thorium, it will sink its differences in the common cause of keeping its factories going.

What the scientist is saying is that within three centuries the sources of energy on which our present civilization is based will be approaching depletion.

The case with the second element, the substance with which physics works, is not much different from that of energy. Many of the sources of our essential materials are being depleted in this rich country, and we are now importing some that we formerly exported. At the present rate of use in the face of increasing demands we should find ourselves bankrupt of our key materials at about the same time we are bankrupt of our accustomed form of energy. Looking back three hundred years, we see that physics played its role in the midst of increasing plenty; looking forward three hundred years, we see that it must in all probability play its role in increasing scarcity of both energy and substance.

From the vantage point of the present we see physics appear between the Metropolis of Europe and the Great Frontier, riding high on the boom when conditions were unusual and abnormal — and highly favorable to this science. Thus far it has been a prime creator of the wealth and luxury we enjoy. In reality physics has in all that time created nothing. It has moved things from one place to another and it has fabricated them, but it has not created any substance. On the contrary physics appears as the great destroyer of both energy and substance. In its first centuries — up to now — physics discounted the future for the present to help give us what Vernon L. Parrington called the Great Barbecue, paid for with irreplaceable capital.

In an imaginative exercise let us view physics in the role of fate. A master tragedian might represent it as a character with uncanny skill and evil intent concealed under the pleasing cloak of preliminary good works. Master of a magic formula for combining energy and substance, physics, like the

Pied Piper has lured men on to the luxury and extravagances of the Big Barbecue. But in doing this, it has progressively destroyed the very elements of its own magic. Seeing men turn on one another — as they have been doing since 1914 — for what is left, physics, realizing that its own game is up and that its magic formula can no longer work, ends the play with its supreme gift for destruction, revealing its true character as a destroyer just when the curtain falls on the shattering ruin of civilization itself. By the law of the drama, the main character must see his predicament, he must struggle to avert the disaster, but he is swept along to the inevitable and by forces he cannot control, even though he may have originated them.

Since the tragedy has not yet occurred, except in token form, physics may yet have a choice as to what it is going to do in the time remaining. Historically it is faced with a decreasing supply of energy, a diminishing amount of substance, and the demands of an increasing number of people. It had great success in expanding the booming world of abnormal conditions. What will it do now with a contracting world that is getting back to the normal prefrontier stage? It has known how to act on the false assumption of the infinite and unlimited. How will it respond to the unrelenting facts of the finite?

I have no doubt that the physicists will unfold many new devices, for they still have some time. I am sure that people will continue to say with wistful hopefulness that the physicists will open new frontiers and continue to work their old magic. They, along with their fellow scientists, will indeed be men if they open anything comparable in magnitude or influence to what they, and all of us, had in the Great Frontier.

Fred A. Shannon

The following piece illustrates the waggish side of Walter Prescott Webb.

In 1954 Fred A. Shannon of the University of Illinois was president of the Mississippi Valley Historical Association, while Webb was vice-president. Customarily, the vice-president was to introduce the president at the presidential dinner in Madison, Wisconsin, on April 22 of that year. Ever since Shannon's pungent and penetrating excoriation of The Great Plains, younger historians — and some older ones — had lined up behind one man or the other and had dreaded the moment these two would come face to face. Accordingly, the banquet room was filled.

Webb is a sober speaker who drones clearly and doggedly in a voice without highs or lows. He was well into his speech before many of the audience realized its — and Shannon's — leg was being pulled. Then they sat back and enjoyed themselves hugely. When Shannon arose to begin his talk, he prefaced it by saying that he hadn't realized the extent of Webb's devotion to him but that he was going to retain his objectivity.

"*I still contend that Webb is all wet,*" Shannon said, "*but I am willing to submit that wetness of any sort in a Texan is refreshing!*"

At that, Shannon, who would have made a perfect "heavy" in the old stock company days, cocked one eye at Webb and smiled impishly. The audience roared.

"I think Shannon and I did more to restore the historical profession to a sense of proportion that night than anything that had taken place in years," Webb said later. "We didn't dodge the fact that we had differed, but we also showed 'em that men don't have to agree to be friends and to respect each other."

J.B.F.

❧❧

MEMBERS OF the MVHA, Ladies, and Gentlemen:

I do not know when in my whole career I have approached the task of introducing a speaker with any greater desire to do a good job than I have tonight. I have known the gentleman I am to introduce for a number of years and have come to have a profound respect for his varied abilities. I have seen him perform under circumstances which would have suited me just as well had they been otherwise, and in that performance I came to admire the tenacity with which he stuck to his position and the skill with which he defended it. As for my part, I would have preferred to withdraw from the field, but since we were in it together, and he showed no disposition to withdraw, I did not have the heart to forsake him. And so we both stayed to the end.

The gentleman who is to address you is in my opinion a dual personality. You know him best as a historian, a man thoroughly versed in his chosen field of economic and social history. I will not describe the contributions he has made because they are standard and you know them as well as I. He was born in Missouri, the home of some other good men, educated in Indiana and Iowa, and has taught in Kansas and Illinois. He was Pulitzer Prize winner in 1929 for his *The Organization and Administration of the Union Army*, published in 1928. His latest work is *The Farmers' Last Frontier*. So much for the historian.

I know him who occupies the seat of honor here tonight best in his second role, that of a critic. And if anybody ever sets up a Pulitzer Prize for criticism, or an endowed chair of criticism the speaker tonight will have good claim to several ex post facto awards. For my money he'll get the high job. I trust that if you did not know it already, you have begun to suspect by this time that I speak on this subject with authority. As a matter of fact, my knowledge of the speaker's skill and ability as a critic is intimate and has the validity of a primary source.

In the beginning of my experience in gathering information on the subject, I thought that the gentleman really meant all that he said. I took him quite seriously, and it required some time for me to realize that what at first struck me as sharp and rather acidulous comment was in reality a form of humor, a game, an intellectual method of joking. Of course I knew that we joke only with people we really like, and when I got to this point I suddenly saw something that I had not seen clearly before — that this man likes nearly everybody, and me probably more than most.

I reminded myself of the Mexican musician in San Antonio who tried to defy the famous mayor, Maury Maverick. When Maury Maverick became Mayor, one of his first official acts was to bring the tamale queens back on the plazas, and the Mexican musicians who played stringed instruments for the visitors and tamales — he brought them back too. The Mayor enforced strict sanitary codes with the food venders and required the musicians to wear the picturesque Mexican hat, the red serape, and bell-bottomed gold-braided trousers. Maury would, like Theodore Roosevelt, go at night scouting the city to see that the regulations were being observed, that San Antonio was being true to its tradition. On the plazas where the braziers were glowing, where tangy odor of tamales and chili again filled the air, Maury saw a very tall handsome Mexican guitar player without the required uniform.

As many of you know, Maury Maverick is built somewhat on the order of a bench-legged bulldog, low on the ground, and he often has similar manners. He looked up at the tall Mexican and said:

"What in the hell are you doin' out here without a uniform?"

"I," said the Mexican in broken English, "am exercising my constitutional rights!"

This answer floored the Mayor temporarily, but when he recovered, he gave unmistakable and emphatic orders, and for Maury to be emphatic is to be very emphatic indeed. In about thirty minutes the guitar player showed up, hat, serape, bell-bottomed striped trousers — the whole works. Maury heard him say to his companion: "The Mayor he like me; he joke with me." And so I say about the speaker. He has joked with me.

Tonight he comes as the historian, not as the critic.

Ladies and Gentlemen: I present to you my friend, your President, Fred A. Shannon.

Fields of Common Interest

I
AM NOT very well informed as to the purpose of this program and did not know until yesterday that I shared with Mr. Germany* the responsibility of laying the predicates for the panel discussions that are to follow. As I understand it, this conference was initiated by the business groups, and the question naturally arises as to what their purpose is. The title, "General Education for Business Leadership," furnishes a clue suggesting that business is in need of leaders, and that it is turning to the universities to see if they can do anything to supply leaders. This university is flattered by the gesture, and will, I am sure, do all in its power, in keeping with its character as a university, to be of service.

As a matter of fact the University has for a long time been rendering a service to all segments of Texas society by turning out trained people in many specialized trades and professions.

An address before the Education-Industry Conference sponsored by the National Association of Manufacturers, Southern Humanities Conference, and Texas Manufacturers Association, Austin, Texas, April 1, 1954.

* E. B. Germany, president of the Lone Star Steel Corporation.

Each spring, at commencement or before, representatives of business organizations appear with very large nets to catch the trained young men and women as they fall off the educational assembly line. I wish to emphasize that the nets are spread to catch those trained and specialized in the trades and professions. The preference of business for these trained and specialized graduates has had, and is having, a profound effect on university programs.

There is another group — rather small in number and rather select — who at the present and in the immediate past have been rejected, thrown back as it were into the pool. These are the people who have devoted themselves to getting a general education. They have not learned a trade, they have not gone in for a profession, they have not become specialists. They are not prepared to fit in as an interchangeable part, as a cog exactly like thousands of others who help make up the intricate business machine of today. These are the people who in defiance of the highly practical considerations have elected a general education, have chosen to satisfy their driving curiosity to understand the world they live in, to know what it was like yesterday, why it is what it is today, and to guess intelligently at what it may become tomorrow. They have the ability, or should have it, to assemble data, use judgment in evaluating it, and they make a habit of trying to see things whole. They are among our very best students, but when they graduate there is often no place they can go with any assurance that they will be wanted or needed. As a matter of fact, they often feel that they have made a terrible mistake in pursuing a general education.

Now I return to the topic before us. *General* education for business leadership. Is it possible that you gentlemen of the business world have found that you may have a place for educated people as well as for trained ones, that you are ready to experiment with intellect, that you are willing to give hostage to culture? I note that this discussion breaks up into three panels, and that the topic of each panel sounds highly academic: Communications has to do with the English language, speech and writing; History is concerned with the past, which is dead for those who do not know it; and Foreign Languages have to do with the manners, customs, and speech of such outlandish folks as Germans, French, Spaniards, and Portuguese.

I am not informed as to who set these three topics up, but it is perfectly obvious that each one has something more than an academic interest to the modern business corporation. The world, and even Texas, has become far more sophisticated than it was fifty years ago. Business organizations want their letters and reports in literate English. Every company must expect its officials to make public speeches, and these speakers lose no prestige with their company or their clients if they perform with clarity, reason, and charm. As for foreign languages, we all know that most businesses, certainly those that support the NAM, are international in scope; we also know the advantage of being able to carry on business relations with a foreign people in their own medium of communication. As things stand we are among the great nations almost illiterate in the foreign language field. We speak anything but English poorly and we write it hardly at all. My conclusion is that business, in seeking to encourage the language, written and spoken, and to improve its proficiency in two or three foreign languages, is serving its own end. It is asking the universities to do what they have been trying to do since universities were established. As for business history, the third topic, it lies so nearly in the field of business that the question of its relation hardly need be raised.

The subject assigned to Mr. Germany and me is entitled

"Fields of Common Interest." It seems to me that I have touched on these fields of common interest. If the business-men are under the auspices of the NAM concerning themselves with *general* education, then they have established a very important point of overlapping interest. General education is the concern of most of the members of the University faculty who are on this program. They believe in general education, and no one will be more delighted than they if it turns out that those students who pursue general education will not be rejected by employers as impractical dreamers. If business has an interest in either of the three fields assigned to the three panels, then we have three other points of overlapping interest.

The question is sure to arise: Where in the complicated university structure should business turn to find people who have this mysterious *general* education? Primarily, you must go to the one division or college which has been all but sub-merged under the amazing growth of the so-called practical schools, colleges, and divisions. I refer to the College of Arts and Sciences. It would indeed be a great thing, in the opinion of many, if through changed circumstances businessmen find it to their advantage to come to the rescue of what actually is the very heart of the whole educational system in the true sense. Other divisions and colleges may train, but only the College of Arts really devotes itself to the function of promoting general education.

Let me tell you some things that are happening to the College of Arts and Sciences:

1. It is used as a preparatory school by the professional and trade schools that have grown up in recent years around it. In most cases, if not in all, these specialized groups set forth the most rigid prescriptions as to what their future students must take. Also, they tend to draw the lines tighter and

tighter, leaving the student less and less opportunity to pursue his intellectual interests, satisfy his curiosity about literature, history, or philosophy. The College of Arts and Sciences was the original university, but it is being cut away by these professional and trade-school abrasives.

2. The student who pursues general education in the College of Arts and Sciences, who is not preparing for something else, suffers a loss of prestige. As the society is made up, it is difficult for him to justify his lack of practicality. It is a little unfashionable for him to admit that he has an insatiable curiosity to know and understand the world around him before he goes out into it. The social climate is unfavorable.

3. The business climate is also unfavorable, as I have already indicated. When he goes into the business office to get a job, he is likely to be asked "What can you do?" If he were to answer "I can think" he would be ushered out. He is not likely to be queried about literature, philosophy, art, or history, probably because the man who is querying him knows little of these things himself.

4. Finally, the College of Arts and Sciences is now in full retreat before the overwhelming forces that surround it. Therefore it tends to adulterate its own program, decrease its requirements, and adopt substitutes.

I am not enough of an idealist to believe without further proof that business as represented by the NAM has come here for the purpose of rescuing a sinking institution and saving something that must be of value to our society. On the other hand I am enough of a realist to believe that business has recognized that something is wrong somewhere, that business is not getting a certain type of individual that would be very valuable to it and its purpose. I shall be delighted to have evidence that business is toying with the idea of hunting for educated people on the chance that they might in time be worthy of their hire. They do not need these people to tend machines, throw levers, or punch time clocks. They may have need for those who will want to understand the whole operation, see relationships between the various parts of the organization, and that have some knowledge of the society which the business serves. They may need people of courage and vision, and maybe they are not finding them under the present operation.

Here in the College of Arts and Sciences can be a great and rich field of common interest. I understand that this conference is the first of a series projected for this university and others. This evidently means that the NAM is quite serious in its program of examining *general* education as a source for providing leadership in business. I shall assume that it is serious, but my observation leads me to believe that this is something of a new interest, and to me a most encouraging one.

A closer examination of the printed program shows something very strange. You will recall that I have been talking on the gown side about the College of Arts and Sciences. I have intimated that this College of Arts and Sciences has been neglected. I wish to amend that and say that the sciences have not been neglected, either by business or government. The neglect has been of the Arts. Turning to the program, I find the word Humanities, and I note that this conference is built around the non-sciences, mainly around the humanities and related subjects. We must conclude, then, that business has not found in the professional or trade schools or in the highly specialized sciences exactly what it is now looking for. If this is not true, then why is this conference pitched at the humanities?

I do not know exactly what the humanities are supposed to be, but in general I understand that they concern themselves with human beings and their relations with one another. It is no secret, I think, that the humanities along with their kindred subjects generally known as social sciences have been in bad repute. It was quite all right to study rust in oil pipes, the tensile strength of fiber, and the stresses and strains of sky-scraper construction, but a little risky to examine the canker of society, the tensile strength of poverty or the stresses and strains of human maladjustment. Anything in the name of science goes in the inanimate world, even with plants and animals, but he who speaks or writes about human affairs must be very careful. I trust you will pardon me if I make an observation on the panel programs set up here. They are good as far as they go, but they are all concerned with the tools that businessmen need as much as they need their merchandise and machinery. You want your people to write clearly, speak convincingly, and know languages so they can communicate with foreign customers. There is nothing in this program calculated to alter anyone's view of society. There is no philosophy, no economics, and very little history. I mention this because I think it very important to understand at the beginning the extent and nature of our common interests. We would like to know whether you are looking for more "practical" tools for business to use, or are you seeking people who have a well rounded view of the society in which we live, and of the human relations therein.

In conclusion I would like to state the possible advantage of having a few people of general education in any first-class business organization of any magnitude.

1. There are distinct limits to which the carefully trained and narrowly specialized person can rise before he runs into serious obstacles. The ceiling for a broadly educated man of equal mental ability is considerably higher. He — the educated man — is not confined to shop talk, and when he gets

to a certain level, he is thrown with educated people who want to discuss literature, music, philosophy, government, and economics. We have all seen the competent person who became ill at ease when the conversation got out of his narrow range, and such a person almost automatically checks himself out of further promotion. He is a good $10,000 man, but he will not likely be chosen for the $40,000 job. He simply doesn't have what goes with it.

2. The too highly specialized man finds it difficult to see his organization whole, all its parts in relation to one another. What is more important, and much bigger, he does not see the relation of his firm's business to the society in which it must live. He may not even see the relation that should exist, and now does exist, between labor and management. He is likely to make serious mistakes when he speaks for his company to an informed public. I will illustrate with an example.

Two summers ago I was invited with representatives from forty other universities and colleges to attend a Du Pont conference at Wilmington, Delaware. Each day the head of some division came before the group to explain the working of his division. These were top men, but so far as I could make out, most of them had had only technical training. This particular program had to do with the manufacture of the two fibers, Nylon and Dacron. We had just returned from the Nylon plant where synthetic cotton (Nylon), cut to one-and-one-quarter-inch staple, was being made and baled in 500-pound bales exactly as we bale cotton. One of these bales was falling off the line every two or three minutes. As I watched this marvelous process, I asked myself what effect it would have on the cotton and wool growers of Texas, the South, and West. So in the conference next day I asked the man in charge a question.

I explained why the problem bothered me. My question

was: "What can I say to the cotton growers and wool growers of my section as to the effect this marvelous high-speed production of synthetic cotton and wool will have on their economic future?" He was a little nettled, and obviously had never given any thought to the social consequences of what he was doing with such efficiency.

"You can tell them," he said finally, "to do what the mule raisers and horse growers did when the automobile and tractor came in."

There was immediate consternation among the high officials who were present. Three of them, including the chairman of the board of directors and one vice-president, came to me and apologized for the man's answer. Three days later another official asked for a place on the program to read a paper he once wrote dealing with the problem I had raised. He said: "I want to assure Mr. Webb and the other members of this conference that we have given consideration to the problem."

It may be that the highly trained man who first answered my question told the truth, but from the point of view of the Du Pont company he gave a poor answer. Had he been educated in the humanities, history, and economics he would have known the answer and would have handled himself much better. My guess is that when it comes time to select a new director, vice-president or president, men who must meet educated people, the decision will be to leave this man where he is.

Finally, I want to say that this may well be a memorable occasion when an academic group and a business group sit down at a table to find their common interests. We on the academic side need much from business, and it may be that business needs something that we have to offer. At any rate it is something that we have sat down together, and I trust we may do it again.

For Whom the Historian Tolls

After Webb's *Mississippi Valley Historical Association* presidential address was published, *American Heritage* asked him to write an article on how historians write. Webb delivered the following article in which he flayed his brethren in the guild for their failures with the art of history.

"*I guess I made it too strong,*" Webb commented later, for *American Heritage* turned it down. Webb refused to modify or soften. He still thinks historians should take stock of themselves. Here is his stocktaking.

J.B.F.

❧❧

IN THE JUNE, 1955 issue of *The Mississippi Valley Historical Review* I had an article dealing with the training of American historians. I pointed out that about the turn of the century the professional historians, in their zeal for the so-called scientific method of arriving at historical truth, divorced themselves from the reading public. They lost, perhaps irrevocably, their general audience, the public and the general reader, in a cloud of academic dust. I said that a bold experiment was now being made to recapture the lost audience, that *American Heritage* had collected some three-quarters of a million dollars as evidence that people were willing to read history, and that the present anxiety of the editors was whether the historians could write it — in such a way as to keep the subscribers coming.

The editor read the article and requested me to comment further on the point stated. The point is a brutal one, and can be phrased best in three questions: Why can't historians write? Or if they can, why don't they? Do they scorn the general reader or do they lack the art and the skill necessary to reach him and hold him?

The historian will be defined as the person who has adopted history as a profession and makes his living primarily by teaching it. He is assumed to have an advanced degree and to be occupying a chair in a college or university. This is indeed a narrow definition, and fortunately does not include the scores of writers who are excellent historians, and who win more than their share of prizes, such nonprofessionals as Douglas Southall Freeman, Paul Horgan, Tom Lea, Bernard DeVoto, Carl Sandburg, and Arnold Toynbee, not one of whom has or had an earned Ph.D. degree or ever occupied a chair of history.

There may be another group of historians — though I cannot name one — who quit teaching when they found out that they could write. They loved writing — as one must to endure its pangs — and turned to it with devotion. By Gresham's law, the poor writers are left to teach after the good have departed. When Clio, the Muse of History, took off from Olympus, the gods must have gathered around and told her

about what Will Rogers told the president of a denomina-
tional college. Will said: "Dr. Blank, you've got a fine set of
boys and girls here. Learn 'em all you can, but don't learn 'em
too much because if you do, they'll quit being Denomina-
tionalists." If a historian writes too well, he is likely to cease
being a professional historian.

If historians can write for a wide public, why don't they?
When the editors and promoters launched *American Heritage,*
they were careful to place it under the sponsorship of two
important historical organizations of national scope. The
basic idea was to regain the lost audience by presenting history
in palatable form. "Our chief requirement as we set out to
tell about it all (the story of American life) is that the things
we talk about must be interesting." So wrote the editor in
the first bound issue. He got together a most imposing list
of names for the advisory board, and another for contributing
and regional editors, a staff heavily ballasted with big-name
historians who have prestige in the important universities of
the country. Moreover, the editors announced, though without emphasis, the authors who contributed acceptable material would be compensated at magazine rate.

The whole pitch implied that at last historians were going
to be given an opportunity to appear before a wide public,
and to be paid for doing it. They were to have their own liai-
son magazine; the editors — staff, advisory, and regional —
were all friends at the court. The historians were invited to
prepare a feast made up of the choicest tidbits of the past; the
public was invited to attend as paying guests.

The management must have had visions of the electric
effect that the fine scheme was having throughout the land.
The managers could see the lights burning late in the studies;
they could hear the clatter of hundreds of typewriters as the
historians began to prepare their prize dishes for the apprecia-

tive guests; they awaited the avalanche of unfootnoted and interesting articles dealing with the drama, tragedy, frivolity, futility, and pathos of the American past. Managements must have such dreams or they would never be managements.

At last the day arrived when the feast was spread. The guests were there, money in hand, many thousands of them, but the historians remained away, and they still are conspicuous only for their scarcity. The management found itself in a crisis and had to scramble around for some real writers.

Only the editors can say how much of this happened, but there is evidence to be found in the five bound copies of *American Heritage* that have appeared at the time of this writing. The lead articles number from nine to twelve in each issue, with a total of 52 for the five issues. Only eight of these appear to be by teachers of history. The balance are by professional writers, librarians, directors of historical societies or museums, physicians, journalists, advertising men, capitalists, naval officers, lawyers, explorers, and a college president. The editors evidently held back no reserve of historians, hoping to make the second feast better than the first, because not a single historian showed up in the second issue. There were only two in each of the other four. Thus it turns out that professional historians — those engaged in teaching history — constitute only twelve per cent of the contributors.*

It is for the editor to say (if he finds this reminder of his past anxieties interesting enough to print) whether the historians ignored the invitation to write or whether they failed to write interestingly. One guess is that they did a good deal of both, leaving the harried editor no recourse but to turn to others.

* The writer had to depend on the data in the editorial note about authors or on *Who's Who in America* for this classification. It may be that some of the contributors otherwise classified are teaching history, but if so no evidence of it was found in the available sources.

A cursory examination of the standard articles in the high-level historical journals of national scope will furnish proof that few historians exhibit superior gifts of expression. The articles are correct, the sentences usually — after the editors get through with them — are grammatical, and the footnotes are properly right at the bottom of the page. But one finds in them little charm, few vivid figures of speech, and practically none of that soft luminosity — an indefinable quality — which suffuses good writing. The reader may be informed, but he is rarely lured, enthralled, or captivated by the art of the performance.

The editors of these scholarly journals would be suspicious of an article that had the qualities which the published ones lack. The editors are under a gentle but real tyranny of the professors who were taught, and who teach, that there is something historically naughty about good writing. Out of the school of so-called scientific history there arose the idea that a great gulf exists between truth and beauty, and the belief that the scholar who attempts to bridge it deserves to fall into it and drown. The real scholar must choose truth, and somehow it is better if it is made so ugly that nobody could doubt its virginity.

It so happens that the vulgar public loves beauty, a well-turned phrase, a figure of speech which makes a pattern of truth stand out above a ruck of facts. This same public sees no reason why the true should not wear a garment as graceful as that which drapes its opposite. It seems to have turned out that the imaginary gulf between beauty and truth has turned out to be a real gulf between the scientific historian and the public. As a result the professional historian has lost the big audience, and is left to peddle his wares to his fellow historians, who are actually little more interested than the public and not nearly as well heeled, and to young captives in the college classroom.

Historians of the craft may be divided into three classes, those who can't write, those who can but don't, and those who do. The first group may be dismissed with sympathy but without blame. They draw the water and cut the wood and grow gardens around the small colleges and the universities. For appearance sake each one has a project, some book he is going to write, but he never gets around to it because he lacks the inner compulsion that drives the more artistic relentlessly to work. He has become a historian because anybody can do that who can cut wood, or even move it around. There lies the whole past, a big forest, and it takes no talent and little resolution to work in it, gathering dead limbs, making logs, rails, or crossties.

But the real artist can take from this same forest the material out of which he makes a fine cabinet or a graceful chair or a jewel box lovely to feel and to see — and useful too. Each, according to his gifts and industry, can do something where there is so much material; and there is a place for the gatherers of deadwood, but not a high place.

Among those who can write but don't are the lazy who are not willing to pay the hard price, and the perfectionists who never find all the evidence. The teacher in a college does not have to write. He is not paid for writing, and draws his check at the end of the month without doing it. The check may be bigger if he writes, but he would rather have the present one on present terms than to pay the price for a problematically bigger one next year. He is likely to turn critic of those who do write, and convince himself that he could do better than his writing colleagues who are after all rather mediocre fellows and quite superficial to boot.

The perfectionist is the most exasperating and the most frustrated of the lot. He often has superior ability, and insatiable curiosity which becomes a master instead of his servant, and an utter disregard for the flight of time. He is quick to find errors others make, and these strengthen his resolution never to commit that sin. The surest way to carry out the resolution is to do nothing, or to do so little that there is no room for an error to breathe or do any damage.

In the last volume of his *Study of History* Arnold Toynbee addresses himself to this class of scholars with biting sarcasm. "Why," he asks, "has a phobia against taking action [writing] become the scholar's distinctive occupational disease?" On the same subject he says of the scholar who can but does not write because he is seeking the will-o'-the-wisp of omniscience, "To leave his talent hidden in the Earth till his corpse is lowered into the grave to rot beside it is a sin of omission in which criminal negligence swells to the dimensions of high treason. . . . In the incubation of each particular work of art, a human creator's soul has a corresponding period of . . . gestation which it will shorten or lengthen at its peril; and an egg that is allowed to go addled under the suffocating breast of a broody hen will be just as sterile as the still-born fruit of a premature birth." Toynbee thinks that the scholar must be a man of action just as the warrior and the businessmen are. Not only should he write, but he should publish. "The error, to which scholars are notoriously prone," he says, "of spoiling their work by continuing to revise it after it has reached and passed its optimum state can often be traced to an infantile ignorance of one of the fundamental rules of art." That rule is to know what to leave out, to know that the sculptor does not spare the marble.

Let us turn from the broody-hen historians who addle more eggs than they hatch, to those who for better or worse have their say. If the gulf between the historians and the reading public is to be bridged, if history is to be purveyed to the people in palatable form, this small residue of writing historians is going to have to do the job. In order to do it, they are going to have to forget or ignore a great many things they were taught in graduate schools by professors who are bound by the traditions of historical methodology.

In graduate school the student is taught to select a subject of such small dimensions that it offers no challenge to the intellect, does not develop the mind, and has little or no significance when developed. He is encouraged to write without benefit of imagination, to avoid any statement based on perception and insight unless he can prove by the documents that his idea is not original. He is trained to believe that he can be objective, and that the best way to be objective is to be so colorless as to give the reader something akin to snow blindness. In some quarters he is taught by precept and innuendo that any attempt to be interesting is a dark sin leading to scholarly perdition, that those who receive money for what they write are popularizers, or journalists, and that a textbook writer is the next thing to a prostitute. Many a student comes out of this ordeal so self-conscious and string-halted that he would avoid originality if he met it in the high road. He has been trained — in timidity and self-repression.

The urge to create, the compulsion to write and to consider writing as an art, and the desire to extract a check from a publisher must be very strong to enable the young historian to break the fetters, and set off on an exalted course of freedom which is so essential to any creative work. If he cannot write interestingly, he will not reach the general reader; if he does not write textbooks, he cannot reach any students but his own. His influence will be limited to the few who read his footnoted articles, and to his own students, most of whom regret that they did not get into the class of a better-known man, known through his writing.

The upshot of the business is that history is being served

up to the public largely by nonprofessional historians. They appear on the best-seller lists, are preponderant among contributors to magazines, and win most of the prizes in open contests. It would be a grave error to state that the public has excluded itself by making his ivory tower into a prison, one the public is not eager to break into.

If there be a young historian who would like to break out of the self-made prison, here are some suggestions that may be of use. He should depend on his ability to convince his reader by clarity and vividness rather than by an array of footnotes. He must write with sympathy for the general reader who loves economy of words because he is essentially an artist. He should write to publish, and publish in any medium from the county newspaper to the most learned or slickest popular journal. He will soon find that each piece of published writing gives the writer more than it does the reader. It sharpens his wits, widens his vision, and if it is any good brings opportunity for more writing. Finally, he should not be contemptuous of the publisher's check. These checks have an effect comparable to that which Mr. Dooley said the invention of suspenders had on mankind. Enough of them will turn man loose to work with both hands. There is, after all, nothing more exhilarating to a writer than a publisher's check, and historians do not see enough of them.

Introduction of
President Harry Truman

This introduction was never made. In 1955 The Mississippi Valley Historical Association held its annual meeting at the Hotel Jefferson in St. Louis. Former President Truman was to make one of the dinner addresses. Even though six hundred historians were to be present, Mr. Truman's secretary sent a letter, which arrived the day of the dinner, saying that because of the pressure of work on his memoirs he would be unable to attend. Despite urgent appeals from St. Louis Democrats, from local newspaper editors, from Mr. Truman's Washington office, and from at least one national committeeman that cancellation in such a manner and for such a reason was a breach of manners, to say the least, Mr. Truman remained adamant. The reaction of the six hundred historians need not be described.

Webb did not get to make his introduction. He says that he would like another opportunity.

J.B.F.

❦❦

MR. TRUMAN:

It is a custom, almost an inviolable law, to introduce a speaker to his audience. The assumption is that the audience has little knowledge of the speaker and needs to be told who who he is, what he has done, and what may be expected of him. I cannot act on this assumption tonight. I prefer a truer one, namely, that this audience knows a great deal more about the speaker than he knows about the audience. Therefore, Mr. Truman, I am reversing the customary procedure by introducing the audience to the speaker.

Your audience tonight comprises the members of that profession whose business it is to teach American history to the American people, mainly the youth, and to the world. This is the national organization of American historians. They, and their successors, examine critically all the evidence left by the men who make history and also the evidence left by the contemporaries of the principals. In the long run it is difficult to hide very much from their prying eyes for they have the patience to await the emergence of the documents and the whole truth. In a sense they tend the scales of justice, and see that the makers of history are given honest weight.

It is not often that one of the principals of history appears before this body. Your appearance here tonight is therefore of more than usual importance. You will be listened to with attention, and what you say will be retailed in a thousand classrooms to tens of thousands of university and college students within a week. It is my guess that in this re-presentation you will be dealt with more objectivity than you have sometimes been in the past.

The members of this audience are especially interested in the reports that you are now using your supposed leisure for compiling and writing an account of your own experience in national and world affairs during one of the most tempestuous periods of the past two centuries. We trust that the reports are true, and that nothing interferes with this plan. It is unfortunate that so few of the leading makers of history have had the inclination to record their observations on their own stirring times.

When I heard that you had turned historian, I thought what a fine thing it would be to bring Mr. Truman to the university to teach young people about American political life. How the students would flock to your classes. But when I took a second look at the local situation, I decided that the plan was not at this time very practical. I think I should prepare you for what may happen to you after your performance tonight. Teachers are getting scarce, and many of the members of this audience are here to recruit men of promise. If you do well tonight, you are likely to be offered a job if you will make yourself available. The pay won't be very good, but I'll tell you one thing. You will have the best tenure you have had since you got out of the army.

Finally, Mr. Truman, I want to take advantage of this opportunity to express a personal grievance. In 1948 you caused me to lose a whole night's sleep. My grievance was heightened next day when I read in the papers that you went to bed at ten o'clock. It seems to me that in a crisis like that you should be more sympathetic. The next night I slept fine, but some of the best people in Texas, according to Dun & Bradstreet rating, did not go to sleep for two weeks.

I think I speak for this entire Association, meeting here in your state in the heart of this great nation, when I say that your presence here makes this a memorable occasion.

Ladies and gentlemen: Mr. Truman.

The Historical Seminar:
Its Outer Shell and Its Inner Spirit

I T IS EASY . . . to outline a few external characteristics of
the seminary," wrote Herbert Baxter Adams in 1884, "but
difficult to picture its inner life." * Since Adams wrote
this, more than seventy years ago, a great deal of attention has
been paid to the external characteristics, the outer shell, and
not so much to the inner life and spirit of the historical seminar. I chose the subject for this occasion because the seminar
has played an important role in my own work. In discussing
it with others, I gained the impression that there was something peculiar in my use of this instrument of graduate instruction; and had the results of my experiment been less satisfying,
I might have concluded that what I had was no seminar at all.

Further investigation revealed that I was not quite as original, peculiar, or off-side as I first thought. What had seemed

This paper was presented as the presidential address at the Forty-eighth Annual
Meeting of the Mississippi Valley Historical Association in St. Louis on April
28, 1955, and printed in the *Mississippi Valley Historical Review*, June, 1955.
Copyright 1955 by the Mississippi Valley Historical Association.

* Herbert Baxter Adams, "New Methods of Study in History," *Johns Hopkins
University Studies in Historical and Political Science*, II (1884), 107.

the outer shell soon came to appear as the protective cover for the inner spirit where the vitality exists. My conclusion — which may be stated at the outset — is that the great seminars have been animated and made great not by any method but by the inner purpose, the great program, and the dominating idea of him who conducted it.

The seminar may be defined as a group of mature students or scholars studying and practicing the art of investigation and research under the direction of an experienced supervisor who sets the goal and sees to it that the best-known procedures are utilized by the group journeying toward it. The question arises as to what is the goal, the aim, of the director. What is he trying to do for these young people who have come for help? What, also, is he trying to do for himself? The answer to the first question is simple: the director is trying to help these young people become historians. He, the master craftsman, is trying to make master craftsmen out of apprentices and journeymen. Years ago I read a story of a German *Meister* of the craft of making beer kegs. The master often reminded his apprentices that in his own apprenticeship he made a perfect beer keg. He doubted that any of them would ever make a beer keg as perfect as his had been. He harried them, drove them; he cajoled and bullied them; and in the end the poor apprentices were quite full of beer kegs, and a little tired of the subject. And in time they probably learned that the master's beer keg was not as flawless as he had represented it. But this parallel between making beer kegs and making seminar papers will not be further developed here.

The director of the seminar puts the apprentices through the motions that the historian must make in the production of a finished work. He has them read, collect, analyze, organize; he has them write a paper with preface, outline, notes, and bibliography, and finally present the results of their labor

— their own little beer kegs — for the judgment of the master
and of their fellows. If there is no aim other than this, then
the seminar is a thinly disguised course in pedagogy, the director is conducting a trade school in historical mechanics, and
the seminar is overrated, with more space in the graduate cur-
riculum than its importance justifies.

Those who have glorified this sort of seminar have put great
stress on the use of documents and original sources. Traditionally here is a place where the last shade of meaning is
squeezed out of an official document. There is nothing wrong
in putting a document under the microscope or through the
critical wringer, analyzing it, looking into the bias and prejudice of him who made it. Nor is there anything wrong in seeking the motives of those who have committed great crimes or
performed great services. The ability to do these things is
possessed by many people, notably constitutional lawyers,
probate judges, and police officers. These skills and critical
attitudes can be taught in high school, and have been; they
are taught again in college; they should be perfected by any
student who has an M.A. degree. In the graduate seminar no
student should receive any credit for having them, but should
be penalized if he lacks them. These things — mechanics, procedures, and methods — constitute the outer shell, the indispensable minimum equipment needed by the student to
qualify for admission to the sort of seminar that I am trying
to delineate.

This brings me to the second question: What is the director
of the seminar trying to do for himself? The answer is that he
is trying to push out the bounds of knowledge. He has got far
enough to ask questions, to know what kind to ask, but he has
not found the answers. Therefore, he calls in a group of graduate students, already equipped with method, takes them as
junior partners, and sets them off on the quest for the answers

to his questions. He is seeking aid while giving it. It is his hope that one out of ten will strike a trail, pursue it until he makes a field of inquiry his own, and become transformed into a creative historian. The director knows that he is a gambler, gambling in human possibilities, gambling that out of ten technicians there may emerge one who glimpses an idea and in pursuit of it becomes a master. The other nine will be no worse technicians than they were, and some of them may be a little better for having had pointed out to them a far country which they will never enter. That far country, reserved for the few, is the goal of the director. It has been the goal of all directors of all great seminars. Such seminars have been conducted by curious, restless investigators, bold enough to build a program of inquiry and writing around a compelling idea. With such men, and such men only, is found the inner spirit of the seminar.

In this paper I shall review briefly the origin of the seminar in Europe and its importance to this country and some results — good and bad — of its application in both places. Second, I shall show by example that the great seminars have been given by men with great ideas, men who used the seminar as an instrument of investigation. In the third place, I shall relate my own experience with the seminar.

It is generally stated that Leopold von Ranke of Germany was the father of the historical seminar, and it is assumed that he invented or adopted a new method of pursuing historical investigation. The method was already old, and had long been used in philology and in Biblical study. Ranke borrowed it from philology and carried it over into history, applying it to modern official documents rather than to ancient writs.* He was contemporary with Lyell, Wallace, Darwin, and

* Edward G. Bourne, "Leopold von Ranke," *American Historical Association, Annual Report*, 1896 (2 vols., Washington, 1897), I, 71.

Renan, who were applying the analytical and critical method with startling results in their respective fields. He turned the lecture room into a laboratory, using documents instead of a "bushel of clams." He was trying to make history a science, which has turned out to be as simple as making science history, something the scientists have had too much gumption to attempt.

Ranke's emphasis on documents came at a fortunate time in just the right place and was applied to a favorable period, the sixteenth and seventeenth centuries. Situated in Central Europe, he was surrounded by new national states and others in the process of formation, and in each capital were the accumulated official records as yet untouched by historians. Ranke led the way in cracking these treasure houses to set numerous students off on careers of writing national history based on official documents in an era when the volume of official documents was manageable.* The documents were mainly political, and the histories based on them became almost entirely so. Ranke and his followers accepted Edward A. Freeman's dictum that "history is past politics and politics is present history" before Freeman phrased it. By such procedure, Ranke believed, history could be written *wie es eigentlich gewesen ist*, but we know better now.

Ranke's method was accepted as a sort of historical Geiger counter, and students flocked to Berlin to acquire this new gadget. The results in two countries, Germany and the United States, are worth notice.

In Germany, Ranke built up a school — known as the Ger-

---

* Historians of contemporary times are appalled by the volume of documents. In a lecture in Austin, Texas, April 8, 1953, Arnold Toynbee stated that the British documents pertaining to World War II would fill a shelf eighteen miles long. Ancient historians are handicapped by a paucity of documents, contemporary historians by a plethora. Ranke hit on a period when they were abundant but still manageable.

man school — which numbered not less than thirty historians who attained in their day a considerable reputation, and many of them were distinguished. Most famous among them were Wilhelm von Giesebrecht, Georg Waitz, and Heinrich von Sybel. Their concern with official documents gave them the official view, and they began to tend more and more toward a glorification of the state. Sybel broke away from Ranke, and with the aid of Friedrich Dahlmann founded the Prussian school, which numbered among its members Johann Gustav Droysen and the notorious Heinrich von Treitschke. What they taught by Ranke's method we learned in 1914 and rehearsed in 1941. The study of state documents had led to the worship of the state. Ranke cannot be blamed for this perversion, although it grew naturally out of his basic principle, his belief that by depending on official documents one would arrive at truth as it really is. The Prussian school took the documents and proved to the satisfaction of themselves and many others that the German Empire was the noblest work of political evolution, that Prussia was the crown piece of the Empire, and that the Nordic race, of which Germans were the purest example, was superior to all others.* Nothing could better illustrate the danger inherent in any method considered infallible.

The results in the United States were not so fatal. While Ranke was at the height of his power, just before and after the Civil War, Americans began to go to Berlin and other centers, and return to the United States to preach the documentary gospel. They brought back the shell, the idea that they must be scientific, prove every statement with a footnote, that a felicitous style was no longer desirable — nay, it was

* For a treatment of the evolution of the German schools of "scientific" history from Ranke on, see James Westfall Thompson, A History of Historical Writing (2 vols., New York, 1942), II, Chaps. XLII and XLIII. Thompson denies that Ranke himself was objective.

reprehensible — that imagination was dangerous, too thrilling for the pick and shovel brigade of historians. They brought the method but forgot the substance; they brought what was valuable and needed, but some of them — not all — left behind what was indispensable, something Ranke himself had. They did what disciples often do; they warped and distorted the best work of the master.

These returning natives arrived on the American scene at a fortunate time, in the midst of an educational boom when new states were setting up new universities, when history as a university study was new. In 1880 there were only eleven professors of history in the whole country.* Any man who had the prestige of a European degree, and especially a German degree, could get a job. In 1884, these men took the lead in organizing the American Historical Association, and elected Leopold von Ranke the sole honorary life member. Eleven years later, Edward G. Bourne read a paper before the Association commemorating the hundredth anniversary of his birth.†

The cult spread and the newly trained Ph.D.'s took their Geiger counters into the state and national archives to repeat two generations later what Ranke and his men had done in Europe. They extracted the documents, mainly political, and began to turn out source books of all kinds. The movement culminated when Albert Bushnell Hart launched the "American Nation Series" in 1904, and, to use his own words, drove a team of twenty-four historians through the field of American history. These volumes were fairly uniform in style, uniformly dull, heavily documented, primarily political, highly factual, wholly uninspired, and completely divorced from the reading

* Michael Kraus, *The Writing of American History* (Norman, Okla., 1953), 5.
† Bourne, "Leopold von Ranke," American Historical Association, *Annual Report*, 1896, I, 67-80.

public. In them was none of the savage beauty of Parkman, the insight of Macaulay, the vision of Gibbon, or the restrained yet luminous imagination of Jules Michelet, of whom James Westfall Thompson said: "He not only took history for life, he lived himself into the past to an extent unexcelled before or since." * Here was American history with all the blood and guts squeezed out of it. Something that had lived and moved was chopped up into twenty-seven parts so that some 280 years of history could be treated in ten-year blocks. These books had neither the charm of literature nor the exactness of science, and the series is being discarded in favor of a new one equally ephemeral. The conclusion seems to be that in this field of history the method of "science" confers no more immortality than other methods. There is no such thing as immortal history, a way of saying that there is in history no permanent truth; the facts may be permanent, but their meanings are in flux, and the historians only guess at them.

We have witnessed here the results of the seminar in Germany and the United States. The Germans perverted its use with such skill that they led their country down the road to destruction. When the Americans followed the method without imbibing the spirit, they bored the public to extinction. In the land of its origin, the method led to the devil; in the land of its adoption, to dullness. A mighty venture is now on to recapture the lost readers. Almost 100,000 people have indicated their willingness to try *American Heritage*. The editors have received some three-quarter-million dollars as evidence that the people can read. Their present anxiety is whether the historian can write.

My second point is this: The great seminars that have most influenced historical writing have been given by men with great ideas. These men have shared their ideas and their pro-

* Thompson, *History of Historical Writing*, II, 238.

grams with their students and used the seminar as an instrument for expanding the idea and executing a program. They have used any and all methods, but the exclusive use of any one method, even a "scientific" one, has proved fatal.

The best analogue to the seminar I am talking about is an exploring party bound for an unknown country. At the head of the expedition is the leader, the one on whom success is likely to depend and on whom blame for failure will inevitably fall. This leader has that which makes him the leader — that is, an idea of destination. He does not know that he can reach it, or the nature of the obstacles in the way, or what it will be like when he does reach it, but the idea dominates him and makes him hazard the risk.

He selects carefully from those who volunteer for the adventure, hoping that each has intelligence, skill, and endurance. He calls the crew around him and speaks to them in this wise:

You have engaged voluntarily to go with me into a strange and unknown country. You understand that I am not leading you through a park or meadow to show you trails which will, if you follow them, bring you home. I am leading you where there are no trails; we go to blaze a trail that others may follow. I know the direction but I do not know the way; I know the destination I hope we may reach, have an idea of what we will find there, but I am not sure of anything. I know that we shall pass over high mountains and penetrate dark valleys, that we shall see many new vistas, and even though we do not find what we seek, we will find something — an experience to remember all the days of our lives. One more thing I have to say: We are in this expedition together. The idea is mine, and as I share it with you, I want you to share what you find and what you make out of it with us. The campfire will be the clearinghouse for all.

The director is the leader with the idea of destination, the seminar members are the crew of axe-men, observers, hunters and scouts, front, flank, and rear. The library is the high mountain and the forested valley where inspiring views and depressing confusion alternate. The seminar table is the campfire where the party gathers and each member reports what he has seen and what he thinks about it.

The essential elements of the sort of seminar I am talking about are two: the man and the idea. The important moment in the life of the man is that moment when this idea arrives to possess him and guide his work for a lifetime. In this moment he sees some pattern of truth, real meaning in the miscellaneous facts he has been gathering, and he knows that he has found something neither borrowed nor stolen, something his very own. It is the idea that transforms the mechanic, imitator, or pedant into a creative scholar with a destination and a purpose. The insatiable curiosity as to where the idea leads drives him to prodigious industry and endows him with an energy he never before knew. When the man, the prepared scholar, has received this idea he is ready to become the director of the sort of seminar where students enlist to go on a journey full of adventure and misadventure into an unknown country.

I have used the words "creative historian" and "creative seminar," words which I trust make nobody flinch. Those who do might turn to the etymology of *seminar*. In suggesting this I lay myself open to the charge of redundancy in placing the adjective creative before the noun seminar, which basically means creativeness. The seminar in this country was first called a seminary, but that term has been released to those less concerned with so profane a subject as history. Seminary and seminar stem from the French, *seminarius*, from Latin *seminarium*, pertaining to seed. Seminal comes from French and Latin *seminalis*, French *semen*, again pertaining to or consisting of seed, source, first principle, germinal, originative. There is nothing in the etymology signifying method or manner. Arthur P. Newton, the British historian of the Empire, thus defined it: "A Seminar (i.e., a bed in which to sow the seeds of intellectual effort), is . . . a group of disciples (I don't like the word disciple at all) gathered around a Master and inspired by him in a common field of enquiry." * If anybody wants to use the seminar in a creative manner, he will be on clear ground semantically.

Since the idea is so important in the seminar, I want to discuss that exciting moment when the idea arrives; when the idea and the man unite to transform an undifferentiated learner into a dynamic scholar.

Leopold von Ranke's name is synonymous with the "scientific" historical method, but I have never heard anyone speak of his basic idea, his main purpose, or the amazing program of investigation that he carried on for sixty years, resulting in fifty published volumes. He was not an imaginative man; he seemed to evolve slowly from his first task based on a compact body of documents through the history of the popes and of the national states of Europe, culminating his work with a World History, which he completed shortly before his death. One might think he never had that fine moment of insight to set him off on his course and give direction to all he did. I find evidence that he did have that moment, and that it came to him at the age of thirty. In February, 1825, he wrote to his brother: "I am now studying later modern history. Would I might be a Moses in this desert to strike and bring forth the

* Margaret M. Spector, "A. P. Newton," in Herman Ausubel, J. Bartlet Brebner, and Erling M. Hunt (eds.), *Some Modern Historians of Britain: Essays in Honor of R. L. Schuyler* (New York, 1951), 293.

water which is certainly there." * Surely here was a man making ready to set off into a desert — a desert of documents — to see if he could emulate Moses in the act of creation. Since he was working with documents, a documentary method was the natural one, incidental to his purpose and materials. "Der Stoff brachte die Form mit sich," he said in commenting on the Venetian papers.† The stuff not only determines the form, but it often determines the method.

That Ranke used his seminar to further his program is clear from the following passage:

> I am still astonished at the talent and application of the young men who gathered around me. . . . In this circle the work throve. We came upon the Chronicon Corbeiense, whose spuriousness I first recognized without being able to prove it. The members of the seminar made the investigation which proved its falseness.‡

As we leave Ranke, I would like to pose this question: What made him in his day the leading historian of the world? Was it primarily because of the method he taught or was it because of the vast program he carried out?

Other men have been clearer than Ranke in nailing down the moment of synthesis spoken of by Fustel de Coulanges,§ the moment of insight which transforms the student with a head full of inert knowledge into a dynamic scholar with a destination. Augustin Thierry spoke of this moment which led to his *History of the Conquest of the English by the Normans.*

---

* Quoted in Bourne, "Leopold von Ranke," American Historical Association, *Annual Report*, 1896, I, 72.
† Bourne, I, 73.
‡ Quoted in Thompson, *History of Historical Writing*, II, 188.
§ Fustel de Coulanges is reported to have said: "It requires years of analysis for a day of synthesis."

One day [he said] when reading attentively some chapters in Hume, I was struck with a thought which appeared to me a ray of light, and closing the book, I cried, "All this dates from a conquest; there is a conquest at the bottom." Instantly I conceived the project of remaking the history of the English Revolutions by considering them from this new point of view.*

Thierry describes the ecstasy with which one who has had this moment of synthesis works. He said that he devoured many pages to extract a single phrase or a word, and in the process, he said,

> my eyes acquired a faculty which astonishes me, and for which I can not account; that of reading, as it were, by intuition, and of falling almost immediately on the passage that ought to have interest for me. . . . In the species of ecstasy which absorbed all my internal faculties . . . I had no consciousness of what passed around me. . . . The officials of the library and curious visitors came and went through the hall; I heard nothing, I saw nothing; — I saw only the apparitions called up in my soul by what I read.

But of all the accounts of how an idea, an obsession if you prefer, transforms a man, that of Heinrich Schliemann, who excavated Troy and the tombs of Mycenae, is to me the most remarkable. Schliemann was not exactly a historian, never had a seminar nor taught one, but had he done so it would have been a good one. His inspiration did not come in a flash, but had its beginnings, as is often the case, in early childhood, when he conceived the idea of finding the lost city of Troy and excavating it.

* Thompson, *History of Historical Writing*, II, 230.

If I begin this book with my autobiography [he wrote], it is not from any feeling of vanity, but from a desire to show how the work of my later life has been the natural consequence of the impressions I received in my earliest childhood, and that, so to say, the pick axe and spade for the excavation of Troy and the royal tombs of Mycenae were both forged and sharpened in the little German village in which I passed eight years of my earliest childhood.

The chain of events which made him one of the most original scholars of the modern world had its origin not in a document but in pure legend of his home village, a legend of buried treasure. In a pond near his home, legend said, each midnight a maiden rose from the water bearing a silver bowl; in a nearby burial ground a robber knight had buried his child in a golden cradle; and in the garden of the village proprietor other treasures were hidden underground. "My faith in the existence of these treasures was so great," said Schliemann, "that whenever I heard my father complain of his poverty, I always expressed my astonishment that he did not dig up the silver bowl or the golden cradle, and so become rich." This was the first step.

The second step came on Christmas Day, 1829, when the eight-year-old boy received his father's present, Georg Ludwig Jerrer's *Universal History*, published the year before. In the book was a picture of the massive walls of Troy, but Schliemann's father told him that the picture was an imagination, that no trace of Troy existed, that none knew its location. This the boy could not believe.

"Father," I retorted, "If such walls once existed, they can not possibly have been completely destroyed; vast ruins of them must still remain, but they are hidden away by the dust of ages." He maintained the contrary, whilst I remained firm in my opinion, and at last we both agreed that I would one day excavate Troy.

The third step came at the age of sixteen when Schliemann was clerking in Theodore Huckstadt's grocery store, where one day a drunken sailor entered reciting the Homer he had learned before being expelled from the gymnasium for bad conduct. Schliemann says:

He recited about a hundred lines of the poet, observing the rhythmic cadence of the verses. Although I did not understand a syllable, the melodious sound of the words made a deep impression on me, and I wept bitter tears at my unhappy fate. Three times over did I get him to re-peat those divine verses, rewarding his trouble with three glasses of whisky, which I bought with the few pence that made up my whole fortune. From that moment I never ceased to pray God that by His grace I might yet have the happiness of learning Greek.

By the time he was ready to excavate Troy he had mastered English, French, Dutch, Spanish, Italian, Portuguese, Russian, Polish, Modern Greek, Ancient Greek, Latin, and Arabic — thirteen languages in all.

The fourth step came five years later when, at the age of twenty-one, the youth landed as a ship-wrecked cabin boy to become a clerk in Amsterdam at £32 a year, half of which he spent on his studies. He knew it would take money to ex-cavate Troy. There were no great foundations like those around which we timid scholars now flutter like candle flies; and had there been such, he would have stood no chance for a grant. Therefore, he made the money with which to excavate Troy. In another twenty-one years, at the age of forty-two, he retired as indigo merchant to Russia and gold merchant to the mines of California with a fortune. He wrote:

> Heaven continued to bless all my mercantile undertakings in a wonderful manner, so that at the end of 1863 I found myself in possession of a fortune such as my ambition had never ventured to aspire to. But in the bustle of business I never forgot Troy or the agreement I had made with my father . . . to excavate it. I loved money indeed, but solely as means of realising this great idea of my life.

Five more years passed before Schliemann got to Troy, and then, between 1868 and his death in 1890, he not only found and excavated the lost city of Troy, but also Ithaca, Mycenae, Orchomenus, and Tiryns.*

This story illustrates the power of an idea followed by resolution to overcome and burn down all obstructions between the owner and his goal.

Let us now look at some American historians who conducted seminars, and try to determine whether they became notable because they followed a method or an idea. It is often stated that the first seminar was given by Henry Adams at Harvard, but this is an error. The first seminar was given by Charles Kendall Adams at the University of Michigan in 1869 when Henry P. Tappan was president.† I have found little record of what went on in this seminar or of its results.

The case is different with Henry Adams at Harvard, where

---

* This account is based on Arnold J. Toynbee, A *Study of History* (10 vols., London, 1934-54), X, 12 ff. Any historian who is hesitating to take a chance on an original idea should read Toynbee's last volume, which bears the title, *The Inspirations of Historians.*
† Kraus, *Writing of American History,* 165.

he was an assistant professor from 1870 to 1877. It is quite easy to attribute all his merit to the fact that Adams spent some time in school in Germany, and to the fiction that he there learned how to conduct a seminar and became a great historian because he had mastered the latest wrinkle in German method.

An Adams is never a favorable witness for any Adams, but if we can trust Henry's own testimony, he never attended a seminar, knew little about history, and had no use for method. Here he tells of his activities after reaching Berlin in 1858:

> Within a day or two he [Henry Adams] was running about with the rest to beer-cellars and music-halls and dance-rooms, smoking bad tobacco, drinking poor beer, and eating sauerkraut and sausages as though he knew no better. This was easy. . . . The trouble came when he asked for the education he was promised. His friends took him to be registered as a student of the university . . . and they led him to his first lecture.
>
> His first lecture was his last. The young man was not very quick . . . but he needed no more than one hour to satisfy him that he had made another failure in education, this time a fatal one. . . . He had thought Harvard College a torpid school, but it was instinct with life compared with all that he could see of the University of Berlin. The German students were strange animals, but their professors were beyond pay. The mental attitude of the university was not of the American world.*

Instead of continuing in the university, Adams entered the gymnasium, which he spoke of as a public school attended

* Henry Adams, *The Education of Henry Adams: An Autobiography* (Boston, 1918), 75.

by boys of thirteen. He described this experience as a horror, and the school as "something very near an indictable nuisance." In the spring he left for good, and here is his description of his farewell: "He realized what a nightmare he had suffered, and he made up his mind that, wherever else he might . . . seek for education, it should not be again in Berlin." * He further stated that "he had revolted at the American school and university; he had rejected the German university; and as his last experience in education he tried the German high school. The experiment was hazardous." † Of the university he said: "Neither the method nor the matter nor the manner could profit an American education." ‡

On his return to the United States after the Civil War, Adams found a gap of a thousand years — the medieval period — open at Harvard. President Charles W. Eliot, gave him the job against his wishes and at four dollars a day. He said that "when he took his chair and looked the scholars in the face, he had given, as far as he could remember, an hour, more or less, to the Middle Ages." §

It is interesting to know what procedure Adams, the most nearly perfect American historian, followed. He has told us in these words:

He frankly acted on the principle that a teacher, who knew nothing of his subject, should not pretend to teach his scholars what he did not know, but should join them in trying to find the best way of learning it. The rather pretentious name of historical method was sometimes given to this process of instruction, but the name smacked of German pedagogy, and a young professor who re-

* Adams, 81.
† Adams, 77.
‡ Adams, 76.
§ Adams, 300.

spected neither history nor method, whose sole object of interest was his students' minds, fell into trouble enough without adding to it a German parentage. . . . Nothing is easier to teach than historical method, but, when learned, it has little use.*

Adams said he selected as his victims a half-dozen intelligent boys and started them reading whatever they pleased as a background for law. There must have been something about Adams that touched them off, for he says:

The boys worked like rabbits, and dug holes all over the field of archaic society; no difficulty stopped them; unknown languages yielded before their attack, and customary law became familiar as the police court; undoubtedly they learned, after a fashion, to chase an idea, like a hare, through as dense a thicket as they are likely to meet at the bar; but their teacher knew that his wonderful method led nowhere.†

In view of this evidence, and it is a primary source however unreliable, no one can attribute Adams' greatness, as a conductor of a seminar or as historian, to methodology or to German training. I have not found that the self-depreciatory Adams ever admitted that he had that moment of illumination which determined the way he would go. The only obsession he admitted was the futile pursuit of an education.

Though something called a seminar had been given at Michigan and at Harvard, the institutionalization of this device in this country occurred at Johns Hopkins. Here, in 1876, was established a real university as distinguished from such colleges as Yale, Princeton, and Harvard, fortunate in that it

* Adams, 302.
† Adams, 303.

was not cluttered up with undergraduates. Johns Hopkins was a graduate school from the beginning, the only one then worthy of the name. Its reception amazed its founders; its instantaneous success astonished all. Of it Sidney Lanier, in his "Ode to Johns Hopkins," said:

> So quick she bloomed, she seemed to bloom at birth,
> Fore-seen, wise-plann'd pure child of thought and pain,
> Leapt our Minerva from a mortal brain.

A more prosaic writer has said: "To look through the list of first students at the Johns Hopkins University is to obtain a preview of the men who were to become the distinguished members of the faculties of American universities in the thirty or forty years that followed." * Within ten years, sixty-nine men had received the Ph.D. degree, and all but thirteen had positions in thirty-two universities. Among the early fellows are such names as Walter Hines Page, Charles Lane Poor, John H. Latané, Herbert Baxter Adams, John Spencer Bassett, W. W. Willoughby, Josiah Royce, John Dewey, and Woodrow Wilson.

The mortal brain that launched this educational meteor was Daniel Coit Gilman, the first president. That he thought men of ideas should outrank men of methods is made pretty clear in his statement of purpose:

> It misses its aim if it produces learned pedants, or simple artisans, or cunning sophists, or pretentious practitioners. Its purport is not so much to impart knowledge to the pupils as to whet the appetite, exhibit methods, develop powers, strengthen judgment, and invigorate the intellectual and moral forces.

* W. Carson Ryan, *Studies in Early Graduate Education* (New York, 1939), 32.

Again he said:

> In forming all these plans we must beware lest we are
> led away from our foundations; lest we make our schools
> technical instead of liberal and impart a knowledge of
> methods rather than of principles. If we make this mis-
> take we may have an excellent *polytechnicum*, but not a
> *university*.*

The first historical seminar was set up at Johns Hopkins by
Austin Scott at the time George Bancroft was writing his *History of the Formation of the Constitution of the United
States*, published in 1881. Scott was acting as Bancroft's assistant, and the seminar was put to work on the problem. I
quote Herbert Baxter Adams:

> The seminary had the feeling that they had been ad-
> mitted to Mr. Bancroft's workshop, and that, by the ex-
> amination of his materials and his methods, they were
> being taught the art of constructing history. The very
> manuscripts which Dr. Scott had prepared while collect-
> ing and sifting facts for Mr. Bancroft, were shown to the
> seminary. Questions still unsolved were submitted to
> Johns Hopkins students for their consideration, in com-
> pany with their instructor. . . . The feeling was thus en-
> gendered that, in some slight ways, the seminary was con-
> tributing to the great volume of United States history.†

Here again we see the students assisting the director on a real
program of scholarship.

In 1876, Herbert Baxter Adams returned to America with
a Heidelberg Ph.D., and became one of the first fellows at

* Ryan, 29.
† Herbert Baxter Adams, "New Methods of Study in History," *Journal of Social Science*, XVIII (May, 1884), 251 ff.

Johns Hopkins. I suspect that the seminar he later established would rank at the top in terms of what came out of it. His first idea was to continue to study the Roman and German origins of community life, but this soon proved to be impracticable, and he turned to American Institutional History. His students ranged far and wide over the United States, writing about American institutions.

Need I follow the careers of Edward Channing and John Bach McMaster and answer the question as to why students flocked to their seminars and considered it something to remember that they had studied with such men? Was it their methods or their prodigious program of work that made these men worth while? Need I answer the same question for the man from Portage, Wisconsin? * Did he come back from Johns Hopkins to send his name and influence around the world because he had learned mechanics or because he, by looking at his own rude environment, had hit upon a seminal idea which fascinated those who worked with him and set many off on quests to the frontier to create a school of thought?

In 1901, Herbert E. Bolton, a recent graduate from the University of Wisconsin, was exiled to the province of Texas to teach elementary history to the reluctant sons of cowboys. He brought no idea with him, but picked one up on the borderland he had entered, where Anglo-American met Latin-American, English met Spanish, Protestant met Catholic. The archives were at hand, but he could not use them because he knew no Spanish. Deciding to devote himself to the Spanish borderlands, he studied Spanish under Miss Lilia Casis and set to work. He later went to California, where he inspired, and sometimes made a little dizzy, his many disciples who have filled the chairs of Latin-American history all over

* Frederick Jackson Turner (1861-1932).

the continent and beyond. In addition, he turned out a volume of work, which if not prodigious, is quite respectable.*

Another Californian had a somewhat similar idea long before Bolton. Hubert Howe Bancroft, like Schliemann, Walter
Leaf, George Grote, and James Ford Rhodes, took time out
to make money before turning historian.† The regular guild
like to depreciate Bancroft because of his method, that of
hiring better-trained historians than he was and paying them
with the money he knew how to make. Thus he got the title
of Clio Incorporated. He never had a seminar, never studied
method but he evolved a compelling and expanding idea
which would give him no rest. Though historians are reluctant to admit him to the guild, they must concede that he put
the scholarly world into his debt, and that his books, with all
their faults, will outlive the "American Nation Series," old
and news.‡

In all these examples from Leopold von Ranke and Henry
Adams to Herbert Bolton and H. H. Bancroft, we find one
common denominator. It is not a method, but the presence
of an idea or an obsession which creates a driving energy and
an insatiable curiosity. In each case where the seminar was
used by these men, it was used as a creative instrument to
assist the director in extending the area of knowledge.

I speak now of my own experience with the seminar. In my
entire life I have had only two ideas which I consider to have
any originality. I am here tonight because I followed those

* Kraus, Writing of American History, 286-87.
† For an account of the business activities of Schliemann, Leaf, Grote, and
Rhodes, see Toynbee, Study of History, X, 145 ff.
‡ John W. Caughey, Hubert Howe Bancroft: Historian of the West (Berkeley,
1946) vii, says: "In the historiography of the West, no name is written larger
than Hubert Howe Bancroft's." For Bancroft's account of his method see The
Works of Hubert Howe Bancroft (39 vols., San Francisco, 1882-90), XXXIX.
This volume was also published separately as Literary Industries: A Memoir
(New York, 1891).

ideas, without much regard for method, using that which would facilitate the pursuit. Each idea has resulted in a book. A new seminar was organized around each idea shortly after its arrival, maintained until the book was published, and then abandoned. No idea, no seminar.

The first idea, embalmed in *The Great Plains*, came on a stormy night in February while I was reading in preparation of an article about the Texas Rangers for a magazine sponsored by a crooked oil company intent on fleecing the public. I was writing the article for three reasons: I knew something about the Texas Rangers; I was on an instructor's salary; and the crooked oil company paid well until it was rudely interfered with by a United States marshal. Months of research preceded the exciting incident of that night, the moment of insight and synthesis when the miscellaneous facts I had gathered formed a pattern, fell into place, and took on meaning, that moment when something triggers the mind loaded with what Toynbee calls inert knowledge, and brings understanding.

The Colt revolver, which had often been used as a precipitant, always the favorite weapon of the Texas Rangers, was the grain around which the idea formed. I suddenly saw the six-shooter as the natural weapon of the man on horseback, of men moving in an open treeless country where there was grass for horses and cattle and room in which to ride. I saw that in weapons a revolutionary change took place where men left the wooded country and entered the treeless land, where men mounted horses to do their traveling, their fighting, and their work. I had as yet practically no proof of what I knew, but I found it shortly and in abundance, and wrote the story of the historical significance of the six-shooter — I called it the American revolver — which was accepted by *Scribner's Magazine* before I had ever taken a seminar.

But more important than that, I now had a bigger question
to ask: What other changes took place where men left the
forest to dwell on the plains? Nobody could answer that question which had not been asked before, but the question would
not go away, and I had to go to work and answer it myself.
The big question broke up into smaller ones. Where timber
and grass meet, what change took place in geology? What in
botany? In zoology? In anthropology? What in the laws of
land and water? What in literature? Having specialized in
history, I lacked education, knew neither geology, botany, nor
zoology, little anthropology, nothing of law, and not much
more of literature. Hitherto I would have been appalled had
anyone suggested that I explore these formidable subjects.
Yet my curiosity about these suspected changes was such that
it acted like a fire to burn away the obstacle of complete
ignorance. I studied all these subjects in so far as they threw
light on the questions. Geology and law came hardest, but
were quite rewarding.

Because of that quest I understand what Thierry meant
when he spoke of the ecstasy of search, of being insensitive
to what went on around him, and of reading as by intuition.
I could read for my purpose a dozen books a day, and it came
to the point where anything pertaining to the Great Plains
would jump out of the page at a glance, just as Thierry
described.

I was authorized to offer a course on the Great Plains. I
did not rate a seminar, and I did not know enough to lecture.
I said to the class: I think something important happened to
ideas and institutions when men left the woodland to live on
the plains in middle America. Will you help me find out
what happened to this and that and the other? I surrepti-
tiously converted this class, and succeeding ones, into a
seminar — into hunting answers to my questions. My stu-

dents were good hunters. As Henry Adams said, they scurried about like rabbits; they dug holes all over the Great Plains.

It is difficult to remember how much I stole from them, but I cannot forget that I stole something. One student described the Great Plains as a strange land where the wind draws the water and cows cut the wood. Another explained the collapse of the early farming settlements by saying that in the East civilization stood on three legs — land, water, and timber. In the West, two of these legs were withdrawn, and civilization was left to stand, or topple, on one leg. I took that.

There is evidence that the students got from me and from their fellows something in exchange for what they brought, an understanding of the significance of things hitherto without meaning. This evidence comes in letters containing newspaper clippings on subjects we explored. Students sent specimens of barbed wire, pictures of windmills, and occasionally an old six-shooter. Though nearly twenty-five years have passed since the seminar ceased, the letters and specimens still come.

About ten years elapsed between the stormy February night when the apparition appeared and the hot July day when the book was published. Practically nothing but the *Scribner's* article was published in that long interval. Fortunately, I was in Texas, where the ideals of high-pressure scholarship had not then obtruded. Nobody told me I ought to produce, write articles, get in print whether I had anything to say or not.* I had time to mature what I was about, to do what I

---

* Here I wish to say a word on behalf of young men, especially in the large universities, who are driven to write when they have nothing to say and are fired if they do not say it with documentation. The system is vicious and is providing an oversupply of beer-keg makers. I have devised a substitute system for universities to consider. That would be for the university to pay a flat sum to the young teacher for his services as a teacher and put him on a piece-basis for his so-called production. This would require a scale, a bonus system which would automatically register the worth of the harried young man and relieve his superior from making decisions.

had been preparing for since I was carried to the sun-blistered plains of West Texas at the age of four, and where I saw at an impressionable age everything that is in the book except Indians and irrigation. The Indians had just departed, and the water was never there.

The second idea, of greater magnitude but less originality than the first, came to me one spring morning in 1936, and like the first it came when I was working on something not closely related to it — another case of serendipity. Two years later I organized a seminar around the idea, and fourteen years still later the seminar ended with the publication of a book. The central question this time was: What effect did the uncovering of three new continents around 1500 have on the civilization that discovered and for a time owned the continents? Again the central question broke up into specific ones. How did the sudden acquisition and subsequent development of all this new land affect the individual? How did it affect such institutions as absolutism, democracy, slavery, and religious polity? Did it do anything to economic practice and theory? Thirteen years elapsed between the time the idea came and the time I began to write, years of alternating exaltation and misery. Avenues of inquiry radiated in all directions, to new stars in a new hemisphere of astronomy, to the botanical gardens in Europe, to seekers after windfalls of New World gold and silver or hides and fur, to the ensuing booms and bubbles, and to the economic theories and political philosophies that men made to rationalize an unseen revolution.

Let us say that the base pay for teaching is $4500. In addition here is what the young man gets for production: full-length book, $500; monograph, $100; book review $15; paper before learned society, $25. For evidence of recognition by his peers, apply this scale: favorable review of his book, $10; unfavorable review, 50 cents; quotation by another author, $5 each; reference in footnote, $2 each; listing in bibliography, $1. All rates would be doubled for foreign publications. This would be a reversal of a system already started of taking from the scholar all he earns outside his salary, a system which I trust will not spread to other institutions.

The young people who joined me on this expedition contributed much to the final result. Their minds were fresh, often they were eager, and they explored far and near. One question I asked was how piracy of the sixteenth to the nineteenth century was related to the frontier. Why did it arise shortly after the frontier opened? Why did it end early in the nineteenth century? Why was it centered in the Caribbean? Three successive students were assigned the subject. The first two returned with nothing — just a passable paper on pirates; but the third found something. Piracy, he said, had headquarters in the Caribbean because the precious metals from the mines of the Great Frontier had to pass that way en route to Europe. Spain owned the mines and would allow no other power in the Caribbean, a closed sea. No nation could break the monopoly. The alternative was to wink at and support all pirates who preyed on Spanish commerce. This England, France, and Holland did, sharing with the buccaneers their good fortune but never their bad. Finally, Spain's monopoly was broken. Pirates were no longer an asset to anybody; all nations turned on them, and their day was over. In the seminar I had spoken of the entrance to the New World symbolically as a golden door. This student suggested, rather shyly, but with some insight, that the subtitle of his essay on pirates might well be "The Thief at the Golden Door." Thus did he wrap his thesis up in a phrase. I have never asked the experts whether we had a proper seminar. I know we traveled together to far places, we worked at exciting tasks, and I think we came to know what Francis M. Cornford meant when he spoke of a "silent, reasonable world, where the only action is thought, and thought is free from fear," and we traveled in "the company of clean, humorous intellect." *

* Francis M. Cornford, *Microcosmographia Academica, Being a Guide for the Young Academic Politician* (3rd. ed., Cambridge, England, 1933), 47.

Postcard

George Fuermann runs a front-page column in the *Houston Post* which consists of anything from neighborhood chitchat to his own philosophical musings. Occasionally he asks Webb to substitute for him. The following example indicates why Webb is not considered an ivory-towered scholar by those nonacademic citizens who look on the word "scholar" as an epithet.

J.B.F.

❧❧

GEORGE FUERMANN writes a sophisticated column for sophisticated readers, but once a year he goes on vacation and calls on about the most sophisticated group of writers in this state to fill in for him at a minimum cost. The only reason he doesn't get H. B. Fox from Circleville is that H. B.'s rates are high.

Last year I wrote on log cabins. Something like twenty-three log cabins were offered George on the strength of my piece. The market was glutted.

This year I'm going to write on guns, ox yokes, and people, with a little poetry and prose literature thrown in.

Ox yokes are very scarce. They are museum pieces. Stanley Walker has an ox yoke which he claims came down in his own family. It hangs over his fireplace in Lampasas, and is genuine. I have hunted an ox yoke for ten years. A friend of mine over at Commerce has just acquired one and is sending it to me and I am so pleased that I want to tell about it. I do not give my friend's name because if I did some Houstonian would go to Commerce and become a nuisance.

Some years ago I found an ox yoke in a combination antique-junk shop on Red River Street run by an antique and gracious Negro. This yoke was new, with rasp marks still on it, fresh from Bastrop County. It was also $5. I paid for it, and then realized it had been made for the sucker trade. "That," I said, "is not a real ox yoke. It is too short." "Yessir," said the merchant. "It is short. You see, it's a one-row yoke."

The only use that could be made of a one-row yoke would be to plow up the row. The appropriate name for this new form, never seen before, would be a Benson yoke.

George said his readers did not like to pursue one subject too long, and to change it often. The subject now is guns. Years ago I got interested in the American revolver, the Colt, and wrote about it in a book. I give a course at the University of Texas on the West, and in that course I give one lecture on the Colt and the part it played in the history of Texas. I tell about the first two models that Colt made, one named "Texas" and the second the "Walker" for a Texas Ranger, Sam Walker, who helped Colt perfect the weapon. These two models are very scarce and very valuable. So in my lecture last week, I offered to give any student who would bring me a "Texas" or a "Walker" an A on the course and excuse him from all examinations. The next morning the papers announced that the University Museum had been robbed, and that the only thing taken were guns from the Goodall Wooten Collection!

The late Frank Rosengren, who established a bookstore in San Antonio, became fascinated with Texas lore, the stories of guns and gunmen. His obsession finally expressed itself in this Texas verse:

> *Just cut him down, boys, we can't leave him hang,*
> *He's ruinin' that fine pecan tree.*
> *I've knowed that tree ever since 'twas a nut*
> *An' it's growed mighty dear to me.*
> *When the wind swings him around*
> *His spurs skin the bark,*
> *An' his weight, it's a-breakin' that bough.*
> *Just cut him down, boys, we can't leave him hang;*
> *Besides he's done spoiled anyhow.*

It is sophisticated outsiders like Frank Rosengren who by their talent give Texas its reputation.

The name of Frank Rosengren suggests books and the people who see them in Texas. All old-timers will recall H. P. N. Gammel of Austin, rare-book dealer. "No," he would tell you, "the book ain't worth what I ask for it, but some damn fool will pay it." Then there was Dr. E. L. Shettles, Methodist preacher and rare-book dealer par excellence. In his last years, after he was eighty, he wrote his autobiography. The last time I saw him he said: "You folks at the University can be a lot of help to me on this book, but there's two things about it that I don't want you foolin' with. One is the thought and the other is the language." Earl Vandale of

Amarillo spent a fortune gathering Texas books, which are now at the University library.

Marvin Hunter of Bandera is known all over America. He has a museum built by his own efforts which thousands see every year. He published *Frontier Times*, which his father founded, and in it appeared much Texas lore. Another Texan who rendered great service was N. H. Rose of San Antonio, who got together the finest collection of Texas photographs in existence. He specialized in famous peace officers and gunmen of the frontier days. His collection is now owned by Ed Bartholomew of Houston, who has a combination bookshop and used airplane parts. Ed is as unconventional as you will find.

Elizabeth Ann McMurray for years ran a personal bookshop. Unfortunately she has now gone to Boston. She may not have induced the Dallas elite to read, but she did cause them to buy books.

Finally, there is Joe Small of Austin, whose boyhood ambition was to be a publisher. He left the University before graduation and formed a company with a friend who had $62.50. Joe had $65, and so became president of the Joe Small Company. He established the *Western Sportsman*, and with the profits from that founded *True West*, the boldest venture that has been made in these parts. Joe Small thought there was a place for a magazine that stuck to the truth about the West. He has had splendid response from all over the nation. He attempted what seemed impossible. He, like all these others, has followed a dream. They are a strange wonderful breed who have made Texas a better land. They all have one thing in common: they have stars in their eyes even if they have little money in their pockets.

The West and the Desert

I N THE MAY issue of *Harper's Magazine*, 1957, I published an article under the title of "The American West — Perpetual Mirage." That article stirred up the biggest furor of anything I have ever written about the West, and I have been writing about it for more than thirty years. When the editor of this magazine requested me to write something for the Great Plains issue, I suggested that he permit me to reexamine the West in the light of the Westerner's reaction to the *Harper's* article. I hope the readers will observe that I said "in the light of" rather than in the heat of the reaction. The heat was considerable, but I shall ignore it; above all I want to make clear that this is no attempt to have the last word with those who criticized what I said in *Harper's*. I trust that those editors and individuals who were irritated or outraged by my previous effort will look at this one with the calmness to disagree without being too disagreeable.

Here I shall undertake to restate the general thesis developed in *Harper's*, summarize the Westerner's reaction as

Reprinted from *Montana, the Magazine of Western History*, Winter, 1958.

expressed in newspaper editorials or in letters, and examine the scholars' opinion as set forth in serious books and monographs. In conclusion I shall try to strike a balance in the hope that all of us may have a better understanding of the country in which we live.

I. What I Said in *Harper's*

MY PURPOSE in writing, "The American West — Perpetual Mirage," was to put on paper what I thought to be a basic truth about the western half of this country. It seemed to me that the idea I had threw a great deal of light on the nature of the West, explained why it is a section apart from the rest of the country, and made clear why it has a set of special problems which call for special solutions. In short, it made the differences in the needs and compulsions of the West understandable.

The basic idea was this: At the heart of the American West lies a vast desert of varying intensity. It covers all or a considerable part of eight states. New Mexico, Arizona, Nevada, Utah, Wyoming, Colorado, Idaho, and Montana. These states I called the Desert States. The six states to the east and the three to the west I called Desert Rim States because they form the right and left flank of the desert, and each has desert or semidesert areas of considerable extent.

What I undertook was to make the desert appear as the center piece, the most prominent feature of that vast country. Other regions — the North and the South — have mountains, or prairies or plains, but only the West has a desert. It is the factor that has no counterpart elsewhere in the country. Therefore, if we would understand the West, we must begin where the desert is most intense and work outward to the rim, asking ourselves how far does the desert influence extend? How much of the influence is felt here in West Texas, in southern California, in eastern Oregon, or Washington?

It is extremely difficult to change the focus with which people are accustomed to viewing their history or their land. The conventional view of the West is from the east, the direction from which the viewers approached it. The West should not be looked at from the outside, but from the inside, from the center. The West is concentric, a series of moister circles extending outward from the arid to the semi-arid, to the sub-humid, and finally to the humid land. If one will take this view, he will see that the desert is the dominant force in shaping, conditioning, or determining much that lies within its sphere of aridity. The drought that invades the Rim States is the breath of the desert, which is all drought; the fertile irrigation valleys are what they are because the desert influence has made ordinary farming too hazardous or impossible. The Great Plains to the east of the mountains are the burnt right flank of the desert. The forests have fled to the mountain tops to escape the desert in the valleys. Once the desert is recognized and accepted as the dominant force in the West, what goes on there among animals, plants, and men makes sense.

It is the desert influence that makes water more important than land in the West. There is an abundance of land, much of it unoccupied because of the scarcity of water. People have collected where the water is, and are making the West an oasis civilization. Cities have grown up where there is water, grown so much, especially in the Desert Rim States, that they are pushing hard on the water supply and many of them are approaching limitations imposed by the exhaustion of the available supply.

I pointed out that because of the desert influence the West is, when compared to the East, a land of many deficiencies. I made an inventory of the pluses and minuses of the West. I said it is short on water, timber, large cities, national industry, organized labor, and that it has few Negroes. On the plus side the West is long on land, grass, minerals, natural wonders, Indians, and orientals. Finally, I said that the West is short on chronology, that its history is brief, a story soon told. I pointed out what the record reveals, that there is as yet no Westerner in the Hall of Fame, not one Westerner out of eighty-six persons there, that only one battle of national importance has ever been fought in any Western state. I called attention to the fact in the *Dictionary of American Biography* the proportion of Westerners is below the proportion of the population, and that the same is true to a lesser extent to those in *Who's Who in America.* I was trying to explain why in the standard American histories less than one-tenth of the space deals with the American West, more than fifty per cent of the land area.

Finally, I said that the deficiencies of the West, most of them imposed by the desert influence, affected the activity and the attitude of the people who lived there. Lacking so much that people beyond the desert have, the Westerner tends to magnify what he has, build it up to large proportions, make much of little. This tendency gives the West a bizarre character in the eyes of the man from a humid land.

In saying all of these things, I was trying to show that the desert exerts an influence on everything, on the people, on history itself. Nothing was further from my mind than to malign the West. It is my country. I grew up on the edge of the desert, and have spent my whole adult life trying to understand it.

The anger the article created throughout the West I attributed to two things. People do not like to have their country's deficiencies pointed out. Whatever the country is like, they do not want its faults noticed, and especially by one they consider an outsider.

The second reason for the violent reaction may be attributed to the fact that I used the word desert when I might have used softer terms such as arid, semi-arid, and sub-humid. These soft words might have turned away a considerable amount of wrath, but I chose to use desert and desert influence because I wanted to drive the central idea home. I wanted the reader to see the desert as a real factor in the Westerner's life. Once they see this, I thought, they will be better prepared to cope with the problems that they cannot escape. Let us now turn to the Westerners' response.

II. What the Westerners Said

THE PUBLIC COMMENT on the desert thesis was not long in coming. It falls into two categories, editorial comment and personal letters to the author or publisher. In most cases I shall give the source of the newspaper and editorial comment and of the senatorial comment, but I shall not give the name of the persons who wrote me privately.

Apparently the editors realized that here they had a splendid opportunity to come out in defense of their own country. Professors are not too popular anyway, and now one had been caught in the act of maligning or misrepresenting the country they all loved. A desert indeed! That could be accepted, but this misguided author had gone on to abuse the people, to say that they were backward, that they couldn't make the D.A.B. or *Who's Who* in respectable numbers.

The Denver *Post* took the lead in the attack. On Sunday, April 28, appeared a full-page editorial entitled "Us Desert Rats Is Doing OKay." The first sentence reads:

> Listen, Dr. Walter Prescott Webb, historian of the University of Texas, you better take off your glasses and your Ph.D. You've picked yourself a fight.

That sentence sets the tone of the whole piece, and nowhere in it does the writer rise far above an emotional appeal to the prejudice of the reader toward a critic of his country. This editorial was distributed widely over the country. A few days after it appeared a reporter on the paper called by long distance for a thirty-minute conversation. He was a very courteous gentleman who had a job to do and I shall not dwell on our discourse.

"Do you think Denver is in the desert?" he asked.

"You would be if it were not for the elevation," I said. "Does Denver have a water problem?" I asked.

"It sure does!"

We wound up talking a little about what to do with Denver's water problem.

The Cut Bank *Pioneer Press* of May 2, in a long editorial entitled "The Professor Dogmatically Defines the Western Desert" does not want Montana included in the Desert States. "There is a western desert but Montana isn't a part of it." There is a section of Montana west of the mountains that enjoys the climate, the rain and the fog of the Pacific Northwest, but the eastern two-thirds of the state is pretty dry. The average annual rainfall, the author says, is 14.59 inches which puts the entire state in the semi-arid class. The great wheat production cited by the author is possible because of new strains of wheat introduced from other desert countries and to comparatively new methods of dry farming evolved in the American West for lands of deficient moisture.

Conceding that Montana is not a desert, it is in great part subject to desert influence. "We are aware," says the author, "that east of the continental divide there are adverse cycles occurring around periods of seven years." Montana is very fortunate in having a large oasis west of the Continental Divide, and in this and in its cooler climate, it differs from some of the other Desert States.

The Phoenix *Gazette*, April 30, entitles its editorial "An Insult to Arizona and the West." The author thinks that

"Webb has a grudge against the West," that "Webb has spent too many years in cloistered academic halls," that his hypothesis is not very original, that he distorts his evidence, that Arizona has the largest Ponderosa pine forest in the nation, that Webb ignores the great growth of Arizona and other Western states in the past decade. If all the above statements were true, and some of them are, the fact should not blind the editor to the fact that the desert influence is dominant throughout the West, that he is in the heart of it, and that the name of the state is an abbreviation of the Spanish *arida zona*, the arid zone. Surely the influence so powerful in Arizona is not limited to that state.

The Salt Lake City *Tribune*, May 13, sounded a unique note in a lead editorial, "West Would Do Well to Examine Its Mirage!" The editor thinks I covered too much territory, that I am an unorthodox historian, that I erred in saying that the desert is rarely mentioned in Western newspapers and "never by Chambers of Commerce," and that the standard of selection used by *Who's Who* should be critically examined. But of the views expressed he says:

This [article] is no "pot-boiler."

The author is on solid ground with his fundamental idea that the West has been shaped, historically and economically, by the great desert at its heart. This should be more widely recognized by every resident of the West . . .

The author reports correctly that the "oasis" cities of the West are plagued by water shortages . . . but the problem is not confined to this region . . .

Dr. Webb drew the most fire with his complaint that the West isn't producing its share of "persons of distinction" . . .

There is danger, we believe, in becoming unduly apo-

plectic or unnecessarily flippant about unfavorable references to this beloved region of ours. It could be that the
critic has pointed out soft spots that need hardening.

Because the people of Salt Lake City and Utah know of the
desert, and have made the wisest use of it, I could wish no better for the West than that the other states would profit by
Utah's example.

The senators in Washington could not resist the temptation
to join in the chase. The article and some of the editorial
comment were inserted in the *Congressional Record*. The
Christian Science Monitor's Roscoe Fleming made the following report of this phase.

> Senator Gordon Allott (R) of Colorado . . . said that
> Dr. Webb really ought to travel the West and get ac-
> quainted with it. Senator Wallace F. Bennett (R) of
> Utah pointed out that a study of the birthplaces listed in
> *Who's Who* and *American Men of Science* showed that
> per capita Utah led all the rest, with Idaho fourth, Colo-
> rado fifth, and Wyoming sixth. He did not, however,
> point out that their present addresses show that most of
> them had to leave home to make careers.
>
> Senator Barry M. Goldwater (R) of Arizona said that
> the West is young, but that one college in Texas fur-
> nished more officers in World War II than either the
> United States Naval or Military Academy. Meanwhile,
> these and other congressmen from the West put many a
> protesting editorial into the *Congressional Record*.

At least one of the senators admitted that he made his remarks before he read the article.

The personal letters fell into two categories, far removed
from one another. An anonymous picture postcard from Denver said: "If you don't like the West why don't you get out of

it? Or is it because you couldn't make good with all those
illustrious Easterners? As for *Who's Who* why pay a bunch
of guys to pass judgment on you? I have 3 in one family who
could be in the damn book but why pay to see your name in
print? I'd sign this but I'm afraid a bird like you might put
this in *Harper's*. Better get back East. Might add, I haven't
seen your name in *Who's Who*." Another writer declared
that he wanted to come to Austin "to spit on your building."
He took exception to the statement that there were comparatively few Negroes in the West, and assumed that I
thought this one of the West's deficiencies. I was only trying
to account for the brevity of Western history, pointing out
that there was no Negro problem in the West for the historians to write about.

The publicity director of a chamber of commerce in
Arizona sent out a five-page mimeographed letter addressed
to the editor. He sent a copy to me with a note in which he
said: "You will understand that I have something of a reputation for being a snide, sarcastic character." I could not give
him much of an argument on the sarcastic part.

A letter from Denver reads:

Yes . . . you accomplished one thing: you got westerners, such as I, to a point where they'd like nothing better than to use you for target practice. I was not provoked
by the commission of certain facts to your article as much
as I was by the omission of others and the further twisting
of what you did put down . . .

What are you trying to do? Create some new kind of
national tension? Northerners will half seriously speak of
how Southerners still rehash the Civil War. You apparently are making a colossal experiment here with some
sort of "East-show-up-the-West" rift in mind . . .

You simply wrote your dissertation thirty years too

soon, sir. The West is still a frontier with unlimited possibilities and challenge for those with the vision to see it. The East offers little that is comparable.

Maybe I drove the desert idea too hard, but my only purpose was to get the Westerner to see what is all around him. It was not intended to create tension, but to establish harmony between an environment and those who live in it as I do.

The second class of letters came from men who have seen the West whole, either literary men or scientists who have been in government service. The following is from a distinguished writer, a man who loves the desert and will not live far from it, preferably in it.

"We have both read your desert piece . . . with great interest, and, as old desert dwellers, go along with it heartily. It could do a lot to mitigate some really dangerous social and economic illusions in the West, and about the West, if only enough would see this central fact, admit that we're not a garden merely awaiting the right year to bloom. But I fear the C. of C. mind is incorrigible. To them numbers are the proof of 'progress' and will be till we all die of thirst. You should have heard me get jumped on some years ago for saying that the water table under . . . had dropped fifteen feet, and that if the town didn't stop expanding, it was going to stop altogether. A mere incontestable and irreversible fact of nature cannot be allowed to dry out their optimism."

Another resident, not content with the trouble I had stirred up, wanted me to make a study of the social and economic results of the West's desert civilization. He thinks it develops a predatory spirit. "Grubbing for a living in such an arid civilization," he said, "has made the law of the fang and the claw the basis of both its social and economic life. Or as Westerners themselves phrase it, we spend three months of the year 'taking' the tourists, the other nine months, 'taking' each other." I thank the gentleman for his suggestion, but must decline this study.

A retired member of the U.S.D.A. marveled at my "temerity to develop the idea in the face of glowering chambers of commerce." In reference to agricultural conferences he held throughout the country years ago, he said: "I kept a pinchart of the members . . . and it was amazing how the rainfall lines showed up. . . . The biggest Western group came from the tier of universities in Minnesota, Iowa, Missouri, Oklahoma, and Texas. There was a thinner series to the west of that, the Dakotas, Kansas, and Nebraska, but from there on west there was practically nothing until one reached the Pacific coast. . . . The water laws of the Western states tell the story, with riparian and prior rights fighting it out. They are having stiff battles right now here [California] between the northern and southern parts of the state."

From a man who has spent his life in conservation work, mainly in connection with forestry, comes expert information on the water problem of the West.

I . . . relate it [the article] to the conservation of natural resources, and the tremendous shift in emphasis over the years — increasing emphasis on watershed management — the increasing importance of recreation including fish and wildlife. Few recognize the results of devastation by fire, overgrazing, and destructive removal of timber. . . . Few realize that soils exposed by overgrazing, with their higher temperatures, greater ground wind movement, evaporation and soil compaction . . . reduce the beneficial effects of precipitation. . . . The Forest Service has protected plots in the Wasatch Mountains over forty years . . . [but] the vegetal cover is no greater than when the plots were established. Maybe it will take a drought such as the one that put the Pueblos out of business in the late 1200's to bring a realization of the importance of maintaining the balance . . . I wish your article could be read — and its implications understood — by more people. . . . *Harper's* is read by the so-called intellectuals, so maybe it will do more good where it is.

In reference to the burden on water in the West, the writer says: "As I have it about 15 per cent of the land west of about the 100th meridian has to furnish all the water for irrigation, industry, municipalities, and other uses. And only the high mountains where snowfall and other precipitation exceed twenty inches are capable of supplying runoff to feed the streams and underground supplies. Water is the limiting factor."

In this connection, Roscoe Fleming in the *Christian Science Monitor*, May 21, quoted the following from a speech Bernard DeVoto made when he was awarded an honorary degree by the University of Colorado in 1948.

Speaking at Boulder, DeVoto said:

We are desert-dwellers. The West is a desert. A human society more complex than that of small migratory herders of sheep and cattle . . . is possible only because of the snow that falls upon our peaks.

We can meet here today, there are lawns on this campus, there is a University of Colorado, there is Boulder, there is Denver, only because the stone fingers of the Rockies reach up to catch and hold the snow . . .

The West is a desert, and we have told ourselves, and the . . . world that we have made the desert blossom as the rose. We have told the truth. But we would be wise to remember every moment that roses also blossomed in

Mesopotamia and Syria and Tunis and Ur of Chaldees —
and they are desert wastes now.

I wish to close this section of Westerners' reaction by
quoting from a letter that touched me deeply. In the *Harper's*
article I was pretty severe on the society that has grown up in
the Nevada desert. The writer of this letter is a successful
businessman who lives in one of the leading cities.

> I thought [he wrote] you might be tolerantly amused
> by the enclosed clipping . . . an outgrowth of your
> article. . . . I, myself . . . enjoyed this article . . . and
> thought it very reasoned — perhaps too true. Neverthe-
> less, I enjoy this country too much to get up and get out.
> I imagine you're happy to remain in Texas, too.
>
> You were quite harsh on Nevada, and it did hurt a
> little. Those of us who have been here several years, en-
> joying its climate, its beauty nestled up against the mighty
> hills, its hometown atmosphere . . . we are apt to forget
> that these things won't be what is noticed by the first-
> time, or casual, visitor. Many of us are blind to the pres-
> ence of the gambling and the heart-break of too easy
> divorce and too easy marriage, having made our adjust-
> ments . . . separate from these elements. We shall be
> content to live here perpetually, in enjoyment of relaxed
> lives amidst nature's grandeur, enjoying good climate and
> reasonably sparse population. . . .
>
> It is hoped that you can see your way to visit — not so
> that you will reverse your thinking, but so that you can
> see some of its beauties and advantages, forgetting, on
> this search, what every other non-Nevadan too readily
> sees.

This was one of the letters I answered. I shall quote a part of that answer in the conclusion of this article, quote it because I owed this civilized man a justification.

III. What the Scholars Have Said

THE AMERICAN PEOPLE have developed to a high degree their gift for ignoring the scholar, and there is no better illustration of this than the West furnishes in reference to its environment. Space does not permit me to cite the opinions of such explorers as Lewis and Clark, Pike and Long; of such statesmen or politicians as Daniel Webster and Jefferson Davis; of such scholars as John Wesley Powell and Willard D. Johnson. All of these men wrote or spoke about the special problems of the arid and semi-arid West. Most of them conceded the desert influence, one of them made a map of it and that map appeared with modifications in textbooks until after the Civil War.

We need not go back to these early findings. Let us inquire what the statesmen and the scholars have done quite recently. We will examine the work of three men, Senator John Carroll of Colorado, Professor Carl Kraenzel of Montana, and Professor Edmund C. Jaeger of California.

Senator John Carroll introduced a bill in the last session of Congress entitled "The Great Plains Administration Act." The Great Plains Administration, to be directed by five men, would be concerned with the special problems in designated portions of ten states, Colorado, Kansas, Montana, Wyoming, Oklahoma, Nebraska, South Dakota, North Dakota, New Mexico, and Texas.

Section 3 of this bill reads in part: "The Congress hereby finds . . . the Great Plains region has distinctive characteristics in respect of climate, topography, and resource use which are substantially different from those prevailing in adjacent regions, and which are particularly marked by alternating extremes of flood and drought."

Article 8 states that "The Administration shall give first priority to the development of plans and programs for relief from, and alleviation of, flood damage and drought conditions recently sustained or now prevailing in the region and for the prevention and control of damage from floods and drought in the future. It shall submit plans to Congress for emergency flood and drought relief at the earliest possible date. . . ."

Senator Carroll is attempting here what Franklin D. Roosevelt did in 1938 when he designated the South as the "Economic Problem No. 1 of the Nation," and instructed the National Emergency Council to "do something about it." It is difficult for this writer to understand why Senator Carroll excluded the rest of the states that fall under the influence of the desert. The problems he proposes to deal with in the Great Plains Administration are common to parts of all the seventeen states of the American West. Senator Carroll is addressing himself only to the right flank of the desert.

The second recent study to be noticed is Professor Carl F. Kraenzel's *The Great Plains in Transition.* This is a sociological study of the ten Great Plains states. The author feels that the region suffers because the people came equipped with Eastern ideas and institutions and have not yet made the necessary adjustments for living in a semi-arid region.

"The need," he says, "is for the people to make certain adjustments and adaptations to the fact of semiaridity. Otherwise the majority . . . must leave the region, and the few who remain will have one of two choices — to live a feast-and-famine . . . existence or to have . . . a standard of living . . . lower than most other parts of the nation." If the necessary adaptations to semi-aridity are not made, the author believes, the region will decline, the nation will suffer the loss of food and fiber and "will have a poverty area on its hands, with a demand for repeated welfare programs and services." Senator Carroll's Great Plains Administration seems designed to carry out the program that Kraenzel suggests.

Kraenzel develops a most interesting concept which he calls "Space as a Social Cost." In the simplest terms his idea is that people live too far apart to have in a high degree the ordinary amenities of civilization. Space makes social relations too difficult and commodities too dear. I saw this illustrated in Montana in 1956 when the people were complaining that they paid more for gasoline than any other state in the Union. The oil companies were trying to explain this high cost in pamphlets distributed through filling stations. Their main argument was that gasoline was high because they had to haul it so far and had so few customers — the cost of space.

As for the desert in the West, I am willing to rest the case on Professor Edmund C. Jaeger's *The North American Deserts*. It bears a 1957 copyright and is an invaluable contribution to anyone who wishes to understand the American West. The author will not offend the most sensitive because he is a scientist, a biologist, and confines his study to the land, the animals, and the plants, with only passing notice of the influence of the desert on human life and human institutions.

Taking the continent as his field, Professor Jaeger names five deserts, locates them, and provides a map of each. They are the Chihuahuan, the Sonoran, the Mohavan, the Great Basin, and the Navaho or Painted Deserts. Two of these deserts, the Chihuahuan and the Sonoran, lie partly in Mexico and partly in the United States. Three of them lie wholly within this country. Altogether they extend into all the states shown on my map except Montana, and into some of the Rim States, notably Texas and California. They blanket Arizona, New Mexico, and Nevada almost completely. Since the author confines the desert to regions having not more than ten inches of rainfall, he takes no account of the surrounding semi-arid country which feels the desert influence.

He says something significant in the first sentence: "Nearly one-fifth of the surface of the earth is made up of deserts supporting less than four per cent of the world's population." Those who believe that the real deserts are found only in other countries should ponder this: "Nowhere in the world is there as great a concentration of different types of desert climate as in western North America." The Great Basin desert is similar to deserts and steppes of interior Asia; Nevada and Utah are like the Russian deserts around the Aral Sea; Wyoming and Montana in certain parts resemble the Gobi; the Mohave is like the Algerian Sahara; the Chihuahuan around El Paso compares with the Karoo in South Africa and the Riverina district of Australia; and the Arizona Upland around Tucson finds its analogue in the Kalahari of South Africa and in the Mendoza oasis desert country of western Argentina.

"All in all," concludes the author, "one who has an intimate knowledge of all parts of the North American deserts will have a good understanding of desert climates in most parts of the earth." Professor Jaeger's book has opened the way for a better understanding of the American West. I would like to suggest that Congress or one of the foundations create a committee to make a comparative study of the deserts of the world in order to learn how we may best solve the problems pertaining to the American West.

IV. A Word to the Westerners

To those who were offended by what I said in *Harper's* I wish to state a few facts about myself and make some final observations about the desert thesis.

I am not an Easterner, but grew up in west Texas on the edge of the desert. For forty years I have been a member of the faculty of the University of Texas, and my whole life here has been spent in studying the American West and the frontier. I have traveled extensively in the West because I love the wild grandeur of the country, its mysteries, its extremes of topography and climate. During the summer of 1955 I spent a good deal of time in the southern Desert States, and in the summer of 1956 I did what few people do, drove the north-south stretch of it from the Canadian to the Mexican border. Day by day I traveled south, through the Great Basin, through the Navaho or Painted Desert, into the Chihuahuan and Sonoran, and all the time I asked myself the question: What gives the West its special character? It has its plains, its mountains, and its slopes to the sea, but none of these is common to the entire region. The thing that binds all together is the great deficiency of moisture. At the heart is the desert, on the right flank the plains and on the left flank the slopes to the sea. The desert exerts a powerful influence at the center and it exerts some influence east and west, on the flanks. The desert emerged in my consciousness on this trip, and I saw the West as I had never seen it before, its unity and its special problems. I felt at last that I really understood my own country.

I put what I saw on paper and what I put down was published. It was not my purpose to offend, though I realize that people do not like to believe that they live in a desert country. I did try to be clear, to make the desert stand out boldly on the Western intellectual landscape. I used simple words, not weasel words, and I designed a pictorial map in which the desert region was made the most prominent part. I wanted to change the focus of the West from the edge to the center where the greatest force exists in greatest intensity.

To those Westerners who deny the desert I wish to submit

a series of questions by which they may judge whether its influence reaches them:

1. Has your country recently been affected by drought?

2. Is there within fifty miles of your home, land too dry to be cultivated without irrigation?

3. Does the city in or near which you live have a serious water problem?

4. Is there any arable land within fifty miles of your home that could be productive if there were water for irrigation?

5. Do you watch with anxiety the clouds that seem to promise rain?

6. Is the surface water supply you have, furnished by mountains that rise at least 5000 feet?

7. Does the sound of rain on the roof affect you emotionally, make your heart come in your throat, make you want to go out in it as an expression of your thankfulness?

8. Does bank credit loosen up in your town after a rain?

9. Have the people in your state ever prayed for rain?

10. Have people in your state ever raised funds for artificial rainmaking either by explosives or chemicals?

If you answer seven of these questions in the affirmative, then you are subject to desert influence. If you answer all of them in the negative, the desert need be of no concern to you.

I wish to close by quoting from my letter to the gentleman from Nevada: "I could write quite an essay on the character of the people of the West, their courage, their friendliness, their integrity. They make up for many of the shortcomings of the land. They have the adventurous spirit, have to have it. If I have forfeited their friendship, it is a matter of deep regret. My purpose was to help them understand their country and themselves."

History as High Adventure

THIS IS the seventy-second presidential address delivered before the American Historical Association. The previous seventy-one were prepared by seventy persons. Naturally, as the game proceeds, the selection of a subject becomes increasingly difficult because the firstcomers harvested the tallest grain, leaving to us later ones the gleaning of well-mown fields. The presidents have dealt with the usefulness of history, with the facts, the fallacies, the vagaries, the science, the philosophy, the content, and with the individuals who support the great-man theory; they have examined imagination, faith, freedom, distinction, religion, and even truth. He who scans these contributions feels that there is little left to say on the more serious aspects of history. In fact he finds in what has already been said a good deal of repetition and a considerable amount of contradiction.

Two rifts I have been able to detect in this cloud of learning, two opportunities not yet pre-empted. The first is in the field

Reprinted from the *American Historical Review,* January, 1959. Copyright 1959 by The Macmillan Company.

of humor. Judging by the published addresses, one must conclude that historians are deadly serious when called upon to
give testimony of their stewardship. There is, so far as I have
been able to find, scarcely a glimmer of humor, hardly a parti-
cle of wit, and rarely a suggestion of an exuberant spirit in the
whole collection. The historian, reading these addresses seventy-five years hence, will see that presidents had much learning, some wisdom, and no fun at all. Since I am not qualified,
either by nature or by inclination, to fill this gap with a little
laughter, I leave that joyous task to a bolder successor.

The second opening, the one I shall enter, lies in the field of
personal experience, of adventure into the wilderness of the
past, that wild country wherein one can be lost for days or
weeks or months, in exploration as exciting as any known to
Argonauts or *conquistadores*; and the lovely feature about this
delirious experience is that the historical explorer moves
among the dangers and hardships with complete immunity
until finally he comes out in print, in point-blank range of the
critics. It does seem strange that the historians have been so
unwilling to relate their personal experience in historical exploration. They have tended to hide themselves in anonymity,
to be impersonal, to give a blueprint of their fragment of truth
rather than the enthralling tale of how it was chased, cornered,
and captured. What I tell here makes no claim to objectivity.
It is designed to be as subjective and revealing as I can make
it, and yet have within as much truth as one can afford when
talking about himself.

Here I need to warn those young historians who flock to
these meetings, apparently in the hope that they will gain some
clue to getting forward in this profession. They are likely to
think that the man who is president may reveal the secret of
how he got there. Presidents in their turn seem to be influenced by what is expected of them, and so they give some-

thing of their philosophy of history which more often than not exhibits how they felt after they got there. While I, as some of my predecessors have done, am talking tonight out of at least one side of my mouth to these young historians, I would tell them, and I want to tell them with emphasis, that if they aspire to occupy this place, they should listen attentively to my story, make notes my education, graduate record, and college career, and then be extremely careful to avoid following the example of one who has done nearly everything wrong. Seeing what I have done, they will know what not to do.

My presence here is one of the most improbable accidents in the history of the profession. I am here in defiance of geography, regionalism, and history. My background is Southern, both my parents being from Mississippi; my home is west of the Big River, and my field of study has been the plebian field of Western America. All my degrees are from a state university, the one in which I teach. I have never taught anywhere else except temporarily. I am one of the few persons who did not have to leave home to get a job. I am an example of institutional inbreeding which frightens all universities save the two that practice it most, Harvard and Oxford.

Of my seventy-two presidential predecessors, seventy were American citizens, one Canadian, and one French. Of the seventy Americans, sixty-three came from the Northern states, two from the South, and five from the West. Patrick Henry's grandson, the seventh president, was elected from Virginia in 1891. I am the only person ever elected while a teacher in a Southern institution. Two presidents were born west of the Mississippi River, but I am the only one of them elected to the office while a resident teacher west of the river.

Though California has furnished five presidents, all of them were transplanted from the East save one who was from England. So if any young man here is ambitious to be president, he should shun the South and avoid the West. The ambitious designer of a charted career should bear in mind that two states, New York and Massachusetts, have furnished thirty-six presidents, one-half of the total, and that the percentage will increase.

I could tell a great deal about my predecessors, that the average age is sixty-three, that two were in their eighties, thirteen in their seventies, thirty-two in their sixties, and two, Jameson and Turner, in their forties. The office has been held by such distinguished people as presidents and ambassadors and by natives of England, Scotland, France, Canada, Scandinavia, and Russia.

When I pointed out to my wife that 90 per cent of the presidents were from the North and suggested that she should be very proud that at last the South had also been recognized, she replied with one of those marvelous flashes of misunderstanding, "I know — they have decided to integrate!"

Since I promised a human story, I will refrain from statistics. It would be highly gratifying if I could say that from a very early age I wanted to be a historian, and that I bent every effort to this purpose. Nothing could be further from the truth. Actually I have never been ambitious in the profession, as witnessed by the fact that I have a poor record of attendance at the national meetings, have served on no committees, written few book reviews, and have never submitted an article to either of the national journals, although a former presidential address was published. This indifference illustrates two points: first, that I never expected national recognition; second, that I have followed my own interest, acquiring in the process severe penalties and an occasional reward.

What I wanted to be was a writer, and I wanted to write not for the few but for the many, never for the specialist who doesn't read much anyway. I wanted to write so that people could understand me; I wanted to persuade them, lure them along from sentence to paragraph, make them see patterns of truth in the kaleidoscope of the past, exercise upon them the marvelous magic of words as conveyors of thought. With this ambition to write I entered college, very late and with little preparation, and here my past caught up with me. I convinced several English professors that I could not punctuate, and they convinced me that I could not write. For years I did not touch pen to paper.

In my junior year I registered for a course called institutional history, taught by a Canadian-born and European-trained scholar, Lindley Miller Keasbey. What he taught was not history, or economics, or anthropology, or philosophy, but a good deal of all these and more. He swept me off my feet, gave me a method of thinking and a point of view which has entered into all that I have done. His patterns were clear, concise, and exciting. I took all his courses and decided that I would become a teacher of institutional history, beginning in the high schools. But when I surveyed the field, as a wiser person would have done earlier, I found that there was no such thing as institutional history anywhere except in the University of Texas. Then I learned that this man was so unorthodox that he was not welcomed to teach in any standard department. To provide a place for him, the authorities allowed him to set up an independent department, and his former colleagues were dismayed when their best students flocked to him by the hundreds. The authorities finally solved that problem and restored harmony by firing him. And there I was, a specialist in a non-existent field of learning.

But on the record institutional history does look like history, enough like it to fool one school board. Thus I became a history teacher with only two elementary courses in the subject. Now, since I was making a living teaching history, I decided it would be wise to learn something about it, and I began taking advanced courses, and finally took the B.A. degree at about the age most take the Ph.D. In the meantime I had made something of a reputation as a high school teacher of history, and had written an article on the subject, and that made me an expert. In 1918 I was invited to come to the University of Texas to conduct a course in the teaching of history so that it would not be given by a methodologist.

The time had come to start work on the M.A. It was necessary to choose a subject, and here good fortune attended me. A series of Mexican revolutions had made the Texas border a turbulent place; James E. Ferguson as governor had made all Texas turbulent. Ferguson increased the Ranger force, and the Rangers went to the border to commit crimes almost as numerous and quite as heinous as those of Pancho Villa's bandits. These crimes were exposed in a legislative investigation led by J. T. Canales. The exposure made exciting headlines in all the papers. I read those headlines and asked myself an important question: Has anyone written the history of the Texas Rangers? The answer was no. I chose that subject and was off on the first lap of the great adventure, to write the history of the oldest institution of its kind in the world. The story led west, to the frontier, to vicarious adventure of the body, and to real adventure of the mind. Though I was not aware of it then, I had found my field.

Trailing the Texas Rangers, who in turn had trailed the ancestors of some of the best people in Texas, was a combination of drudgery and fun. It was my first work with sources, the faded letters and reports of a handful of men standing between the people and their enemies, men better with a gun than with a pen. Though the records were abundant, I did not stop with the records. Like Parkman I went to all the places where things had happened. I sought out the old men, still living then, who had fought Comanches and Apaches, killed Sam Bass at Round Rock, and broken up deadly feuds inherited from the more deadly reconstruction. With a captain and a private I visited every Ranger camp on the Mexican border where there were still elements of danger; I carried a commission and had the exhilarating experience of wearing a Colt revolver in places where it might have been useful. At night by the campfires I listened to the tales told by men who could talk without notes.

Though the desire to write had been suppressed, it had not been killed. One day I sat down and wrote an article sketching the early history of the Texas Rangers, and for the first time an editor paid me the compliment of writing a check in my favor. This was a landmark, the beginning of a long and happy relationship between me and editors. In retrospect I wondered what had enabled me to break the barrier separating academic people from paying editors. Why had my early efforts been rejected? What new element had entered which enabled me to persuade an editor to write a check? The difference was that now I had something to say; I had learned intimately about one segment of life. The subject I had found in my own front yard was one that I could understand as I could never understand such exotic, to me, topics as the French Revolution or Renaissance art. The way led west.

It was during these same years that the oil boom broke in West Texas. It began in my home town of Ranger, a village of one thousand which became a brawling mass of ten thousand in six months. Law and order broke down, the criminal element rushed in to gamble, murder, and rob. Then the Rangers came to run out the criminals and restore local government to the demoralized citizens. This was a formula repeated in town after town as the boom spread. The genuine boom was followed by a bogus one, run by speculators who floated stock promotions to fleece the gullible public.

One of these bogus companies with headquarters in Fort Worth founded a magazine and decided to do a series of articles on the services the Texas Rangers had rendered in cleaning up the oil towns. The editor addressed a letter to the University asking who was qualified to write the story. The letter found its way to my desk, and I began to tell the story of my Rangers at two cents a word. This pleasant arrangement was interrupted by a United States marshal and judge who had quaint ideas about the uses of the mail.

Though I did not realize it at the time, as I tell this story Texas does seem to have been an exciting place. I shall always be grateful to this crooked oil company because in writing articles for it I stumbled on one of the few original ideas I ever had. As a matter of fact up until that time I had never had one.

This idea came to me on a dark winter night when a heavy rain was rattling on the roof of the small back room where I was trying to write an article for the oil magazine. By this time I knew a great deal about the Texas Rangers, their dependence on horses, and their love for the Colt revolver; I knew the nature of their enemies, primarily the Comanches, and I knew the kind of society they represented and defended. I was ready for that moment of synthesis which comes after long hours of aimless research to give understanding and animation to inert knowledge. What I saw that night was that when Stephen F. Austin brought his colonists to Texas, he brought them to the edge of one environment, the Eastern woodland, and to the border of another environment, the Great Plains. The Texas Rangers were called into existence and kept in existence primarily to defend the settlements against Indians on horseback, Indians equipped with weapons that could be used on horseback. These Texans, fresh from the forests, had no such weapons, for theirs had been developed in the woods and were not suitable for horsemen. While the conflict between the Rangers and the Comanches was at its height, Samuel Colt invented the revolver, the ideal weapon for a man on horseback. It took a year to gather the proof of what I knew that night, and I sensed that something very important happened when the American people emerged from the woodland and undertook to live on the plains. In that transition the Texans were the forerunners, the Rangers the spearhead of the advance, and the revolver an adaptation to the needs of a new situation.

The excitement of that moment was probably the greatest creative sensation I have ever known. With the roar of the rain in my ears, I went to the front of the house to tell the most sympathetic listener I have known that I had come upon something really important, that I was no longer an imitator, parroting what I read or what some professor had said. This idea that something important happened when the Americans came out of the woods and undertook to live on the plains freed me from authority, and set me out on an independent course of inquiry. One question I asked over and over, of myself and of others: What else happened? What other changes took place in the manner of living when thousands of westbound people emerged from a humid, broken woodland to live on the level, semi-arid plains where there was never enough water and practically no wood? This question attended me in all my reading, and led straight to the books I needed. In this chase the Texas Rangers, formerly so exciting, became dull and prosaic fellows, and I cast them aside to follow the new trail that still led west. The teaching of Keasbey came back in full force as I studied the Western environment and tried to find its effects on human beings.

Though I had picked up the M.A. degree in transit, I still lacked the accursed Ph.D. The pressure to get it was gentle, for that was a tolerant age, but it was there, and I was advised to go elsewhere for graduate work. This is wise advice for most people, but it came near being fatal for me. I was already too old, and what is more, I now had an idea of my own which made others — to my teeming mind at that moment — seem of secondary importance. My adviser, Frederic Duncalf, wrote to Professor Turner about a scholarship at Harvard, but Turner replied saying I was too old and should not try Harvard. I shall always be grateful to Turner for this favor and for reasons that will be apparent later. Chicago was less discriminating, and I was fortunate in going where no one offered a course in Western history.

At the end of twelve months I returned to Texas, ill, deep in debt, and without the degree. I would have preferred to omit this adventure, but the academic grapevine has carried the story, somewhat distorted, far and wide, and I dare not ignore it completely. There should be a moral here, but the only one I can find is this: Don't take an original idea into a graduate school.

The trip back to Texas after a long absence is one I shall not forget. At St. Louis I boarded the San Antonio car of the Texas Special, where I heard again familiar voices of people I never knew talking in familiar accents of cotton, cattle, and oil. I was already home.

I brought home some stout resolutions: (1) I would never listen to another academic lecture if I could help it; (2) I would recoup my finances; (3) I would henceforth follow my own intellectual interests at whatever cost; (4) I would write history as I saw it from Texas, and not as it appeared in some distant center of learning. Thanks to the tolerance of my department, I did not have to listen to any more academic lectures. I recouped my finances by participating in a series of highly successful textbooks, a wonderful antidote for academic anemia. Then I turned from textbooks and a small fortune to write history as I saw it from Texas. The road led west, and I now knew I had something to say.

A few people have asked why I remained in Texas, as if that were something needing explanation. The obvious answer should be clear from what has been said. The real answer is that I was bound to Texas by many ties. All the sources I needed were there, and those for the Texas Rangers existed nowhere else. Also the key to understanding the American West up to 1875 was there. It was in Texas that the Anglo-Americans first tackled the problem of living on the plains; it was there that they made the first adjustments, such as learning how to fight on horseback and how to handle cattle from horses. The processes of this adjustment that I was slowly discovering could be perceived more clearly from the south end of the plains corridor than from any other vantage point. And of course when I returned to Texas without the degree I was not in a favorable position to be considered elsewhere. My situation was like that of Mr. George B. Dealey, who began work as an errand boy in a Texas newspaper office and wound up later as owner of what became a truly great newspaper. "Why, Mr. Dealey," an admirer asked, "did you happen to stay in Texas?" "The answer is very simple," Mr. Dealey said. "No one offered me a job."

Without design, I was now on the way to becoming a Western historian. I was excellently prepared because I had never had a course in that field, and therefore could view it without preconceived notions or borrowed points of view. With an instinct for the possible, I had stumbled into the least complex area of the United States where there were no industries as in the North, no special institutions as in the South, no battlefields nor statesmen, and only local politics. Practically all the records were in English so that the language requirements were negligible.

Slight as the demands were, I was ill prepared to meet them.

My idea of the compelling unity of the American West had now become an obsession. That unity was exemplified in the geology, the geography, the climate, vegetation, animal life and Indian life, all background forces operating with telling effect on those people who in the nineteenth century crawled out of the salubrious Eastern woodland to live in this harsh land. To the problem of understanding this Western environment in all its aspects, I applied the technique learned from Keasbey. This technique consisted of taking an environment, in this case the Great Plains, as a unit, and superimposing layer after layer of its components with geology as the foundation and the latest human culture, literature, as the final product, the flower growing out of the compost of human effort and physical forces. There was a compelling logic in the plan for him who would follow it, but to plow through such unknown fields as geology, climatology, botany, and anthropology to arrive finally at the sixteenth century — when men began to make a record of their puny efforts, many failures and few successes — in order to write the heroic and tragic history of the American West was no small task. But it was high adventure. I have never worked so hard or with such exaltation as in those days when I carved out of the books piece after piece and found that they all fit together to form a harmonious pattern which I knew beforehand was there.

Yes, this was the easy field. No matter how hard I worked, I was still a Western historian. No one understood the trouble or the fun I was having in relating the many fields to my topic. In commenting one day to a colleague in a more scholarly division of history, I said: "Never have I felt so keenly the need of an education. The fact that I didn't get one is most unfortunate!"

"Yes," he said, "but think how lucky you were in getting into a field where you don't need it!"

In two respects I was indeed lucky. (1) In the Great Plains

I had chosen an environment simple in structure whose force was so compelling as to influence profoundly whatever touched it. The trail was plain, and the technique learned from Keasbey was applicable. (2) I was also lucky in that I was examining for meaning a familiar land which I had known as a child. A friend asked me once when I began preparation to write *The Great Plains*. I answered that I began at the age of four when my father left the humid East and set his family down in West Texas, in the very edge of the open, arid country which stretched north and west farther than a boy could imagine. There I touched the hem of the garment of the real frontier; there I tasted alkali. I was not the first man, or boy; but the first men, Indian fighters, buffalo hunters, trail-drivers, half-reformed outlaws, and Oklahoma boomers were all around, full of memories and eloquent in relating them to small boys. There I saw the crops burned by drought, eaten by grasshoppers, and destroyed by hail. I felt the searing winds come furnace-hot from the desert to destroy in a day the hopes of a year, and I saw a trail herd blinded and crazy from thirst completely out of control of horse-weary cowboys with faces so drawn they looked like death masks. In the hard-packed yard and on the encircling red-stone hills was the geology, in the pasture the desert botany and all the wild animals of the plains save the buffalo. The Indians, the fierce Comanches, had so recently departed, leaving memories so vivid and tales so harrowing that their red ghosts, lurking in every motte and hollow, drove me home all prickly with fear when I ventured too far. The whole Great Plains was there in microcosm, and the book I wrote was but an extension and explanation of what I had known firsthand in miniature, in a sense an autobiography with scholarly trimmings.

The Great Plains was published in 1931, and no more need be said about it except that it has never been revised, never will be revised by me, never has been imitated, and I am told by the publisher it never will go out of print. I came out of the experience of writing it — doing something in my own way — with a sense of power that comes to him who has made a long journey for a purpose, overcome the hardships, and returned to tell with appropriate exaggeration what to him is an important tale.

I was forty-three years old and still without the degree. There was nothing to do but turn back to the Texas Rangers which had been thrown aside in the excitement of exploring the Great Plains. At this stage Dr. Eugene C. Barker suggested that I use *The Great Plains* as a dissertation and take the degree at the University of Texas. I objected because I thought more of the book than that; it was not a dissertation, and I doubt the subject would have been accepted by any discreet department in the country.* Too big.

It was necessary to go through some mumbo jumbo to satisfy the regulations, but this was done with proper decorum and the degree was given to me a year later. I did not earn it. I have sat on many doctoral committees, always spiritually very near to the cornered candidate, and I have never sat on one where I could have passed the examination. I have, as my colleagues know, I am sure, been a push-over for people who have trouble answering silly questions.

The Texas Rangers was published in 1935, eighteen years

* Apparently Turner had a little trouble in making his Wisconsin subject palatable to the Johns Hopkins professors. Fulmer Mood, after stating that Herbert Baxter Adams directed Turner's dissertation, says: "Adams did not think that the West had institutions worthy of study, but he permitted the young man from Wisconsin to follow his own bent. Institutional history . . . was the style at Johns Hopkins, and Turner wrote . . . on the trading post as an institution. He was able to demonstrate in learned fashion, and perhaps with . . . tongue in . . . cheek, that the trading post could be followed back into Phoenician and Roman times." Fulmer Mood, "Turner's Formative Period," *The Early Writings of Frederick Jackson Turner* (Madison, Wis., 1938), 20.

Dr. Mood is a little unfair to Adams. He accepted the widest variety of subjects in his seminar, including Charles Howard Shinn's *Land Laws of Mining Districts* (Baltimore, Md., 1884), but all had to be treated as institutions.

after I started it. The writing of a book is an act of resolution. At some stage the author must say: "No more research. I will not be lured away by new material. I will write this damned thing now." What led me to this resolution and held me to the task was the realization that 1935 would mark the hundredth anniversary of the Texas Rangers, and the next year Texas would celebrate with fanfare and much false history the centennial of its independence.

Though it takes resolution to begin a book, it takes more to complete it. There are dark moments when the struggling author wonders why he began it, and if it is worth while anyway. There are times when he is lost in the dark forest of alternatives. He can't go forward and he can't go back. Fred Gipson, author of *Hound-Dog Man*, tells a story to illustrate this crisis as he experienced it. After World War I, a neighbor took a contract to drive 3000 head of goats 150 miles through the hill country of Texas. The only help he could get was Fred, aged sixteen, and another boy aged thirteen. The day after the drive started, the autumn rains set in and continued for three weeks. A goat is a self-willed brute, essentially a desert animal, averse to the dousing effect of water and reluctant to travel in the rain. When 3000 goats hump up and refuse to move except under prodding, it makes a problem for the man and two boys who have to move them. The rain had soaked the clothes, the bedding, put out the campfires, and mildewed the food; it had made the soles come loose on the boys' shoes so that they had to be tied on with binding twine and baling wire. Tempers wore thin. The smaller boy threw a stick at a humped-up goat and broke its leg. The boss, completely exhausted himself, lost his temper, and gave the boy the roughest tongue-lashing he had ever had. Fred said he can never forget the picture of abject misery this boy made as he stood, the rain running off his flop hat, his face distorted with anger and hurt, his tears as copious as the rain. When the boss was out of earshot, he made a futile gesture of despair and said, "Dammit, Fred, if I knew the way home, I'd quit." So would many an author.

But if one persists, both goats and books can be delivered. Since *The Texas Rangers* was the only book about Texas that appeared in 1935, Paramount bought it for the Texas Centennial picture of 1936. Paramount made full use of the title, and little else. The picture was quite successful. I am not going to tell you what I got for it in the midst of the depression, but I will say this: what I got made the depression more tolerable.

My next adventure, *Divided We Stand*, published in 1937, guaranteed that I would never be called to a Northern university. I knew this when I wrote it, but I was doing pretty well where I was. The book has been called a pamphlet, a philippic, and a good many other things. Because the people could read it and did, it was not objective. It was based on the simple device of dividing the country into three sections, the North, the South, and the West, and examining the distribution of the national wealth among them. It explained how, after the Civil War, the North, directed by the Republican party, seized economic control of the nation and maintained it through corporate monopoly. The result was that by 1930 the North, with 21 per cent of the territory and 57 per cent of the people, owned and controlled approximately 85 per cent of the nation's wealth, although about 90 per cent of the natural resources were located in the South and West. (I thought of that in examining the distribution of the presidents of this Association. The North has had 90 per cent of the presidents and about the same proportion of nearly everything else.) The book in original form trod on the toes of a powerful monopoly of patents, and it in turn trod on my publisher, leading to expurgation in galley of all reference to this company and to its products, glass bottles. The book was quickly declared out of print on the ground that it did not sell.

But it had done its work. The Hartford Empire Company was hauled to Washington, where I saw the same men who had dictated virtually what I should print about milk bottles quail before Thurman Arnold's young attorneys, who gave an examination that Hartford Empire did not pass. The book was also a factor in causing Franklin D. Roosevelt to issue the report of 1938 and his sensational letter declaring the South the economic problem Number One of the nation, and expressing the determination to do something about what he called the imbalance.

Although declared out of print, the book would not die. The federal investigation of the Hartford Empire Company put all the records in the public domain. From these records I told the whole story and published the revised book myself. It is now in the fourth edition, has sold 15,000 copies, and is still in print. The original publisher is out of business. Recently I re-examined the distribution of the national wealth among the sections to find that between 1930 and 1950 the South and the West gained in every category of wealth and well-being, in some cases spectacularly; and the North, while still far in the lead, lost correspondingly. Now with the Giants and Dodgers in California, with the House and the Senate led and this Association presided over by Texans, it would seem that the North is going the way of the Republican party.

The story of my fourth adventure in history is told in *The Great Frontier*, published in 1952. It, like *The Great Plains*, is based on a single idea, best expressed in the question: What effect did all the new lands discovered by Columbus and his associates around 1500 have on Western Civilization during the following 450 years? What happened to 100,000,-

ooo people shut up in the wedge of western Eurasia when they suddenly acquired title to six times the amount of land they had before, fresh land, thinly tenanted, loaded with resources too great to be comprehended? What did all this wealth and the act of appropriating it do to and for the 100,000,000 poverty-stricken people of western Europe and their descendants?

Slowly the thesis emerged, the boom hypothesis, around which the story was to be told. The Great Frontier precipitated a boom on the Metropolis, a boom of gigantic proportions which began when Columbus returned from his first voyage and accelerated until all the new lands had been appropriated. This boom accompanied the rise of modern civilization and attended the birth of a set of new institutions and ideas designed to service a booming society, chief among them modern democracy and capitalism and the idea of progress. The small booms we know, based on oil or gold or soil, burst when that on which they are based is depleted. They have all been temporary, and the period in which they existed has been considered abnormal. But this big boom, based on all the resources of the Great Frontier, lasted so long that it was considered normal and its institutions permanent. By about 1900 the Great Frontier, of which the American frontier was a fragment, began to close, and as it closed the idea of progress and the efficacy of democracy and capitalism were questioned, put in strain, and since 1914 these boom-born ideas and institutions have been fighting a defensive action. Unless we find some means to restore the boom, future historians may look back on the period from 1500 to 1950 as the Age of the Great Frontier, the most abnormal period in the history of mankind. So ran the argument.

Given the point of view of a Great Frontier set over against the Metropolis, many aspects of modern history fell into

place, could be understood rather than remembered. Under
the controlling idea, or thesis, many subtheses emerged, such
as the windfall theory of wealth, the relation of the Great
Frontier to modern romantic literature as illustrated in Cole-
ridge's "Rime of the Ancient Mariner," the utopias, and such
feats of imagination as *Gulliver's Travels*, Defoe's *Robinson
Crusoe*, and Stevenson's *Treasure Island*, examples of what
the Great Frontier did to the human imagination.

In the realm of economics I advanced the theory of the
dual circulation of wealth, which, if true, might lead the
economists to re-examine their subject and data and their
basic assumptions. The economists have thus far treated
wealth as if it had but one motion, circulation from hand to
hand among the people. Actually, since the discoveries if not
before, wealth has had *two* motions. It circulates horizontally
among the people, and in modern times it has moved vertically between the people and the sovereign, and the character
of its vertical movement has had profound effects on modern
institutions.

By the discoveries the sovereigns of Europe acquired title to
all the lands of the Great Frontier. Unable to use so much
land, these sovereigns began dispersing it to the people, letting
it sift down in townships, leagues, and quarter sections, eventually to small people. This gigantic land dispersal went on
constantly from 1600 to 1900, three booming centuries when
wealth was moving vertically, from the sovereign downward
to the people, making them economically independent and
politically free. When the frontier closed, the sovereign had
nothing more to give, and then he began the reverse process
of taking not from the frontier but from some of the people
in order to have something to give to others. In short, wealth
began making a complete vertical circuit instead of flowing
in one direction. This vertical circulation today supplements
the horizontal circulation so precious to free enterprisers and

keeps it going. If this idea of the dual movement of wealth is true — and it seems obvious once it is pointed out — it should, I thought, have far-reaching implications for the study of modern economics.

The journey through the Great Frontier was a mental adventure of the first magnitude. Many splendid vistas opened, and many things that were familiar took on new meaning. It was lonely there; many times I did not know which way to go, and I, like the boy driving the goats, would have been glad to go home.

As I look back on this program of work, I see in the four books a record of a mental adventure into an expanding world. *The Texas Rangers* was local, simple in structure, and involved little thought. *The Great Plains* was regional, based on a single idea. *Divided We Stand* was national. *The Great Frontier* was international, and, like *The Great Plains*, was the expansion of an idea. The common element in them all is the frontier, dominant in three and present in the fourth. Taken together they tell the story of the expansion of the mind from a hard-packed West Texas dooryard to the outer limits of the Western World.

When one writes of the West and the frontier, the question is sure to arise as to his relation to Frederick J. Turner. It is often said that Webb belongs to the Turner school. I would like to take this opportunity to state my relation to Turner as I see it. No one respects Turner more than I, and no one is less patient with the critics who take exception to some detail in Turner and argue from this small base that his thesis is wrong. There are few so foolish as to say that the existence of a vast body of free land would not have some effects on the habits, customs, and institutions of those who had access to it. That is essentially what Turner said in his essay about the United States, and that is what I said in *The Great Frontier* about western European civilization. Though my canvas was bigger than Turner's, and my span of time a century longer, the thesis is the same. Turner looked at a fragment of the frontier; I tried to look at the whole thing. If Turner's thesis is true, then mine is true; if his is a fallacy, then mine is also fallacious. Since Turner was first in time and I a generation later, I will probably always be counted as a part of the Turner school. And this I accept as an honor.

The question that may arise is this: Am I in the frontier school because Turner led me there or because I stumbled into it independently? I think I stumbled in. I cannot prove this, but I would like to submit the evidence of my assumption.

As already stated, I never had a course in Western history. I never saw Turner. At the time I began writing *The Great Plains* I had never read the Turner essay and I refrained from reading it until I had completed the study. There is little in Turner's writing to suggest that he anticipated the idea developed in *The Great Plains*. The frontier that he knew was east of the Mississippi.

If I did not follow Turner, whom did I follow? What is my intellectual heritage? You will recall that I have paid repeated tribute to Lindley Miller Keasbey, the talented professor of the nonexistent field of institutional history. It was Keasbey who gave me an understanding for and appreciation of the relationship between an environment and the civilization resting upon it; it was Keasbey who taught me, and many others, to begin with the geology or geography, and build upon this foundation the superstructure of the flora, fauna, and anthropology, arriving at last at the modern civilization growing out of this foundation. Turner did not proceed in that manner, but that is the way I proceeded in *The Great Plains* and less obviously in *The Great Frontier*.

But who is Keasbey? To answer that question, we must go

back to the European thinkers who influenced Turner — and
Keasbey. Prominent among them was an Italian economist,
sociologist, and philosopher named Achille Loria (1857-
1943), who wrote in the last quarter of the nineteenth century. Loria's name is found in the Turner literature, and
Turner quoted him in the 1893 essay.*

As an indication that Turner might have found some comfort in the Italian, I quote the following from Loria: "A
tyranny . . . is . . . automatically regulated by the existence
of free land, which of itself renders the exercise of true des-
potic government impossible so long as slavery is unheard of;
for the subjects always have a way of avoiding oppression of
the sovereign by abandoning him and setting up for themselves upon an unoccupied territory." †

The occasional reference to Loria in the literature caused
me to look him up in the library. Imagine my surprise when
I found that the English translation of one of Loria's most
important books was done by Lindley Miller Keasbey of institutional history. If Loria influenced Turner, he most certainly influenced Keasbey, who influenced me more than any
other man. If this is my line of descent, then I am on a
collateral line from the European scholars through Keasbey
rather than from those scholars by way of Turner.

A book dealing with an idea and its ramifications, with a
thesis or interpretation, is more likely to be kicked around by

---

* Turner quotes from Loria's *Analisi della proprietà capitalisti* (2 vols., Turin,
1889), II, 15, as follows: "America has the key to the historical enigma which
Europe has sought for centuries in vain, and the land which has no history reveals luminously the course of universal history." See Turner's footnote, page
207, in the 1893 essay "The Significance of the Frontier in American History,"
in American Historical Association, *Annual Report*, 1893 (Washington, D. C.,
1894), 199-227.
† *The Economic Foundations of Society*, tr. L. M. Keasbey (New York, 1899),
23. Loria published the first edition of this work in 1885. The above sentence
is taken from the revised edition in 1899, the only one available to me.

the critics than one that sticks to the facts, and this may explain why nonventuresome historians, schooled in intellectual timidity, are so factual. Both *The Great Plains* and *The Great Frontier* are idea books, and each has received its share of critical attention. This is to be expected and as it should be. If an idea or interpretation cannot survive a critic, any critic, it is no good anyway. If the idea is sound, then the criticism advertises and spreads it. William E. Dodd told us once never to reply to a critic, and I have never voluntarily done so. The critic is entitled to his view and the author will waste his time trying to change it. The idea has its own destiny, and once launched it is independent of both author and critic.

In conclusion I want to pay tribute to a group not accustomed to receiving it. I refer to several generations of graduate students who have generously contributed their time, effort, and ingenuity in working out the details and ramifications of ideas presented to them in seminar. I have no notion of what they got from me, but I do know that I got a great deal from them, and they a great deal from one another.

They were good companions on some exciting intellectual excursions into the Great Plains and into the vastly greater frontier. Some of them will have their own story to tell and I trust they will have the courage to tell it as they see it, and never as they think I might want it told. I would rather liberate than bind them.

This exercise tonight comes at the end of my academic service. This address is the last act of an official character that I expect to perform, a sort of climax to a high adventure. Because my performance can bring no rewards and inflict no penalties, I have said what I wanted to say in the way that I wanted to say it. If what I have said is unorthodox, it is consistent with much that I have done. I do not recommend my course to others, but it seems in retrospect almost inevitable for me.